R. B. Davis -
from
H. D. Baxter

Christmas 1953 -

This is not your book .

R. B. Davis .

# SOUTHERN
# ACCENT

# WILLIAM T. POLK

# SOUTHERN ACCENT *From*

*Uncle Remus to Oak Ridge*

WILLIAM MORROW AND COMPANY · NEW YORK

*To Tasker and Lilie,*

*Who were of the Old South;*

*To Marion, Marnie and Katherine,*

*Who are of the New South.*

# FOREWORD

This is a book about the South, written by a Southerner out of love, shame, admiration, exasperation, perplexity and fascination.

From Thomas Nelson Page to Erskine Caldwell, the region has been sentimentalized out of existence and debunked out of recognition. I have tried to steer between these extremes. It is not my business to "sell" the South or to reform it, to glorify it or apologize for it. My aim is to understand it, but I confess I am still puzzled by it.

I do not claim that this is any comprehensive picture of the region. I had to leave out many important phases, partly because of physical limitations—"had we but world enough and time"—partly because of ignorance, and partly because of my inability to make a subject, such as education or religion, readable.

If there is overemphasis on North Carolina, that is because the writer's perspective is affected by where he happens to stand.

The South without tears or pedantry is what I have tried to get in this book. The accent is Southern but not unintelligible.

Although I have tried to write about the area truthfully in the main, I must admit that I have on occasion let my natural love of the picturesque divert me from the dull path of veracity. Sometimes I have stretched things. But mostly I have tried to get at the truth, and that is difficult enough, whether for a Southerner or an outsider. I am a Southerner; the South is my land and its people are my people. I love it and them, though there are things about them that I dislike and despise heartily. That makes them all the more interesting to me; I hope it will to the reader.

W. T. P.

# CONTENTS

vii

# PART I

---

## *WHAT IS THE SOUTH?*

# 1

## "Is it True What They Say About Dixie?"

What is the South? It is not what people say it is—and never has been.

From the time of the landing of Amadas and Barlowe on Roanoke Island "in Virginia" to the time of Thomas Nelson Page, say from 1584 to 1884, the region was, by its own admission, "the goodliest land under the cope of heaven," peopled by angels in human form, with a few foreign devils from "up North" thrown in by way of contrast. From the time of Page to that of Erskine Caldwell, William Faulkner and Lillian Smith, the South has somehow become transformed into a never-never, Krafft-Ebing land of psychopathia sexualis, peopled by sadists, masochists, rapists, satyrs, nymphomaniacs, and necrophiles, to mention a few of the better known types, together with assorted murderers, arsonists and lynchers, although it seems to draw the line at cannibalism, even during a failure of the turnip crop.

The notion that the South is a geographical region of the United States of America, populated by rather easy-going people of various shades of complexion, who live rather

3

ordinary lives and get along with one another as best they
can because that is the easiest way, is too fantastic a thought
to be entertained seriously by writers or readers of modern
Southern literature. It is easier and more entertaining to
envision Dixieland as located somewhere between Mt.
Yaanek and Xanadu and to populate it with complexes wan-
dering around in the guise of human characters. The South
has become a cross between a Gothic romance and a Greek
tragedy rewritten by Freud.

We have it on the authority of no less a critic and traveler
than Vincent Sheean that "life in Southern society" is "a
schizophrenic invention without parallel, an insane dich-
otomy from the cradle to the grave." Where did Mr. Sheean
get the evidence for his verdict? From a book by Lillian
Smith called *Killers of the Dream.*

There may be no known method "of drawing up an indict-
ment against an whole people," but it appears feasible to
draft an inquisition of lunacy against them on the authority
of fiction.

To persons who have merely read of the South, it must be
a shock, on visiting it, to discover that the region bears some
resemblance to reality. A few years ago a nonfiction writer
named Leo Lania, in order to gather material for a magazine
article on the South, conceived the original idea of having a
look at the place first, although he was familiar with it by
means of novels, plays, moving pictures and songs. He made
the trip anyway.

After he had traveled as far as Jackson, Mississippi without
meeting a Jeeter Lester or a Popeye, he concluded that he
had got in the wrong region, and he described his reaction as
"bewilderment." On recovering, he wrote: "It is surprising
that so few writers have given us credible accounts of life in
the South. A region only two hours from New York by plane
remains as mysterious as the remote planet Mars."

If so, it is not surprising; it is an old Southern custom to hide behind a paper screen.

The South is largely responsible for the queer notions that people have of it. It has from the beginning fostered extravagant views of itself abroad, and the credulousness of Southerners regarding themselves and their land is as broad as the region itself. There is a tall tale from Warrenton, North Carolina about how a poker game, which was instituted there prior to the Civil War, has been going on continuously ever since, with the eldest sons taking their fathers' places at the gaming table from generation to generation. Of course there is not a scrap of truth or sense in it, but there is a good deal of belief in it. One of the syndicated "believe-it-or-not" newspaper features once wrote me begging for details of the immortal poker game, and I, feeling that such faith should not go unrewarded, supplied it with a long, circumstantial and purely imaginary account of the legendary game, stating that the only interruption in its history was when General Lee visited it, causing the players to stand at attention and salute, but that on his taking a hand, play was immediately resumed.

This bit of tomfoolery, which appeared in various papers, was never challenged, but was taken seriously by a number of people, some of whom wrote me asking whether it was still strictly limited to lineal descendants by primogeniture. I wrote them that unfortunately it was.

Tall-tale telling is not merely an old Southern custom; it is an ancient and honorable American trait. The renowned scientist Benjamin Franklin once wrote a letter to the editor of a London newspaper in which he shared with him this little known tidbit of American nature lore: "The grand leap of the whale up the fall of Niagara is esteemed by all who have seen it as one of the finest spectacles of nature."

Even with the best intentions, the most conservative

Southerners are unable to resist hyperbole. General Lee's chaplain, the Rev. J. William Jones, wrote a book about Lee after the war in which he made this statement: "I think I speak very conservatively when I say that General Lee was the greatest soldier of the war," but he realized that this was a masterpiece of understatement in a region of over-statement, and so he hastened to add, "if not of all history." Southerners saw nothing wrong with that sentence, but Gamaliel Bradford commented: "I wonder what the reverend gentleman would have said if he had not been speaking 'very conservatively.'"

However, he need not have wondered, because what a Southerner would say about General Lee, when not speaking "very conservatively," is on record. While the great man was president of what is now Washington and Lee University, a young lady was accorded the inestimable and unexpected privilege of living in his home. She was, of course, overcome by the honor, but she knew how to express her feelings. "We had heard of God," she said, "but here was General Lee!"

### Trailing Clouds of Glory

Southern fiction really got to work rose-coloring a quarter of a continent in 1832, when Kennedy's *Swallow Barn* fixed the popular conception of the South as one great plantation, "open as an inn and as rich as a castle." Fertilized by William Gilmore Simms, this tradition reached full flower in the 1850's, bathing the South in its balmy and unearthly sweet-ness.

Northern abolitionists contended that all was not perfect in Dixie; *Uncle Tom's Cabin* was published in 1851, and a flood of literature from the self-righteous North was directed against the slavery-propped South. Southern writers, indignantly springing to their pens in defense of their beloved Southland, categorically denied the presence of any imperfection whatsoever.

If the region was "other Eden, demiparadise" before, it became heaven now. To quote Dr. Francis Pendleton Gaines, "houses are almost palatial, social activity is ceaseless, cultured, idyllic; men are gallant, courtly—princely is the favorite adjective—prodigal in the uncalculating Southern fashion; the heroines are beyond description in beauty, sentimentality and the ineffable sickliness from which the maid of romance often languishes."

One would think that the outcome of the Civil War would have shocked the area to a recognition of reality. Not at all. The romantic conception of the South not only survived the war but thrived on it. Mars, after all, was never the god of light. Southern literature ignored the post-bellum South and became reminiscent, an oversight amounting to an artistic crime, for which the region is still paying in the present literary reaction. The South was no longer of the earth, earthy; it was raised in incorruption, trailing clouds of glory.

Southern fiction half a century ago was a fearful and wonderful work of the unfettered imagination; any resemblance to real people, scenes and events was "purely coincidental." The most amateurish novel written in the most excruciating style would, as likely as not, have a foreword ending thus: "This is such a work as Shakespeare or Macaulay might have dashed off in a happy hour of literary excitement. (Signed) Critic."

The following—believe it or not—is a sample of the Southern fiction of some fifty years ago.


### My Day in the Old South

In the orthodox Southern novel of the time, Earl Barringer, the *beau ideal* of manly beauty and the scion of the

wealthy and aristocratic Colonel Barringer, who would
rather die than brook an insult to himself or friend, is awak-
ened by the rosy beams of Aurora and springs from his
couch as he recalls his matutinal tryst with Camilla Montrose, the blooming ward of Col. Fitzhugh Fairfax, his father's
ancient enemy.

Camilla has already reached the trysting place, an oak in
a glade. As she reclines there on the moss in amorous reverie,
listening to the warbling of the feathery choir overhead, she
is hypnotized by a rattlesnake. The reptile charms her with
his basilisk eye. Coiled, he is ready to spring upon the hap-
less maiden.

But Earl Barringer suddenly appears on the scene, and,
throwing his body between the lady and snake, receives the
mortal venom that was meant for his betrothed.

Meanwhile a plot has been hatched by Leopold Cottonmouth Stowe, a disguised ex-overseer, to obtain the fortune
of Colonel Barringer, father of our hero, Earl. Today is the
day of the Camptown races, and Leopold has wagered a fabulous sum with Colonel Barringer that the colonel's mare
Firefly will not win the race. By way of precaution Leopold
has given knockout drops to Snowball, the only jockey who
can ride the fiery Firefly.

This is not the only plot that Leopold has laid today. He
has also laid one against the lovely Camilla. She has re-
jected his addresses, spurned his suit. Repaying scorn with
vengeance, Leopold has forged documents to show that Camilla's parentage is tainted with Negro blood. "We shall see,
my proud beauty!" he mutters over and over to himself
between clenched teeth.

The forged documents, together with the instruments
whereby he committed the forgery, he has concealed behind
a secret panel in the room he occupies as a guest in Colonel
Barringer's mansion.

The hour approaches. All is ready for the Camptown race. But no. Snowball cannot be found. Earl Barringer is having delirium tremens from the gallon of liquor he took to cure the snake bite. Who but the brave and buxom Camilla, disguised somewhat ineffectually as a jockey, volunteers to ride Firefly and save her beloved's father's fortune? 'Tis done! They're off! Nose and nose at the finish! Firefly wins! By a nostril! Camilla doffs her disguise, or so much as is proper. Colonel Barringer, reconciled, takes his enemy's ward to his breast. Leopold Cottonmouth Stowe is foiled.

But not for long. Silently gritting his teeth behind a forced smile, he slinks to the secret panel and opens it to exhibit the forged papers which will wreck Camilla's life.

Zip! A flash of lightning illumines the cloud-darkened room. But Leopold secures the papers and takes them to the parlor where Colonel Barringer, Colonel Fairfax, Camilla and Earl are gathered together.

All are dumbfounded at the news of the terrible taint. Colonel Barringer is about to drive Camilla out into the storm when Earl stops him.

"Hold!" cries he with an imperious gesture. "She is the star of my hope and my future intended."

"My son," says Colonel Barringer, "if you persist in this insane resolve you are no son of mine. I would cut you off as cleanly as I would yon cuspidor."

"Father," retorts young Barringer, "mistake me not. The die is cast. Wealth would be poverty without her love. Poverty would be wealth, if we but shared it together. I would rather marry her, though she worked in a sewing house in New York, than wed the proudest daughter of the highest nobleman of all England, though her brow were decked with a jeweled diadem."

"Boy, you are mad!"

"Follow me," is all young Barringer says.

Leading the way to Leopold's room with the secret panel, he points suddenly to the window on the opposite side. There, mysteriously printed on the pane, is a perfect photograph of Leopold in the act of taking the papers from their hiding place. Earl opens the panel and discloses the instruments of the forgery.

"Curse you!" hisses Leopold. "How did you get that picture?"

Earl, turning to the astounded company, explains how, knowing that Leopold was using the secret panel, he had coated the window opposite with a mixture of quicksilver and buttermilk. The quicksilver acted as a mirror, and the lightning flash, at the same time it revealed Leopold in the act of securing the papers, curdled the milk, thus rendering the reflection permanent.

"We shall meet again, Barringer," snarls Leopold, reaching for his hat.

Earl is tempted to pollute the earth with his vile heart's blood, but stays his hand for the nonce, remembering that there is a lady present.

The storm suddenly subsides, the chants of the mammies and pickaninnies dancing on the levee can be heard above the whistle of the *Robert E. Lee* coming around the bend, and Earl and Camilla are left alone at last.

Earl, beside himself with passion, presses a kiss on the not reluctant cheek of his betrothed. At first blush she is overcome with remorse at her unmaidenly forwardness.

"Oh, God," she cries, "pardon the weakness of woman!" and, burying her face in his bosom, her lachrymal lakes overflowed and anointed his garments with drops which were to him the myrrh of the soul.

"It is pursuit," she sobs, "and not possession that man enjoys, and now therefore the tender regard you have for me

is about to be cremated upon the pyre of my broken spirit
and naught but an urn of ashes left for its memory."

"Never," replies Barringer, "never until God himself is
buried and the dark mantle of oblivion is erected for his
tombstone shall my person or my angel forsake the fair
Camilla Montrose!" [1]

Here let us leave them.


## But Hell Is More Amusing

It took Southern writers a century—say, from Kennedy's
*Swallow Barn* in 1832 to Faulkner's *Light in August* in 1932
—to wake up to the fact that there is more human nature and
drama, and therefore better materials for fiction, to be found
in hell than in heaven, a lesson they could have learned from
Dante at any time.

But once they caught on to it, they went to town.

Southward the star of literature took its way. The roll call
is impressive, with Ellen Glasgow and Mary Johnston in Virginia, Paul Green and Thomas Wolfe in North Carolina,
DuBose Heyward and Julia Peterkin in South Carolina, T. S.
Stribling in Tennessee, Erskine Caldwell in Georgia, Robert
Penn Warren in Kentucky, Majorie Kinnan Rawlings in
Florida, and William Faulkner and Eudora Welty in Mississippi. For good measure the South threw in its *Iliad,* which
is Stephen Vincent Benet's *John Brown's Body,* and its *Odyssey,* which is Margaret Mitchell's *Gone With The Wind.*

No longer did Southern writers fly off to the ends of the
earth as if driven by some centrifugal force—Lafcadio Hearn
had removed himself to a Japanese fairyland, Poe had taken
up his abode in the "misty, mid-region of Weir," and James

---

[1]This concluding dialogue is borrowed practically verbatim from *The
Balsam Groves of Grandfather Mountain* by Shepherd M. Dugger, the only
book I know of that is not like any other book.

Branch Cabell had, by way of Poictesme, got as far as hell.

At last Southern fiction writers began making the attempt to capture the life of their land in a well-wrought mesh of words, to reveal the essential qualities of that life by focusing on its intimate details, and to depict it more as it was than as it was said to be.

Such an attitude takes it for granted that there is no substitute for sight; it calls on the creative imagination to work with its earthy materials and never abandon them. The viewpoint is without condescension or reverence. The life thus brought to light was more rough and robust, yet more varied, subtle and profound than that which had passed for the South in books. Some of these writers, notably William Faulkner, made a desperate attempt to show men and women in their erratic gyrations through this life throwing off, by their collisions with one another, sparks which would light for an enduring instant some wrinkle of the divinely darkened countenance of Truth.

The attempt was made by various writers, but success was very rare.

For a crop of realistic literature, however, the South offered a fertile and fallow field. The life of the South was and is that of the country and the small town. In the city it is practically impossible to see the man for the people, but in town and country the first and great commandment is: "Know thy neighbor as thyself." The pursuit of this knowledge is a fine art, an exact science, the chief amusement and the most popular indoor and outdoor sport of the region. Everything about each resident and the stranger within his gates is seen, noted, discussed and disseminated—everything, including his ancestors, his family, his acts, tastes, habits, faith, idiosyncracies, emotions and motives, how long he says his prayers and wears his socks, what woman he cocked an eye at in church on Sunday, et cetera, ad infinitum.

The drugstore, the Sunday school, the sewing circle, the book club, the bridge club, the courthouse square and all other places are human nature laboratories functioning on the principle that the proper study of mankind is man.

The knowledge thereby accumulated usually goes off in the gas of gossip and is lost, but sometimes it is utilized by a writer sufficiently wise, patient, reckless and unscrupulous.

### What, No Likeness?

Does this mean that a recognizable likeness or portrait of the South is emerging at last? Not at all.

Takes two Southern novelists—Erskine Caldwell, the most widely read, and William Faulkner, the most highly esteemed —and ask: "Is is true what they say about Dixie?"

A great many people must think so. As early as 1950 a total of 23,000,000 of Caldwell's books had been sold, mostly in drugstores, and their number is increasing like the national debt. There is much realistic detail in them, as there is in the paintings of Hieronymus Bosch or Salvador Dali and the stories of the Grimm brothers. Millions of readers doubtless believe that they present an accurate picture of the South, but they do not.

It is true that there are Tobacco Roads in the South, as there are Jeeter Lesters, Dudes, Ellie Mays, Mollies, and Ty Ty Waldens. But the gargoyle is not the building.

In one of Erskine Caldwell's novels, *Journeyman,* a preacher comes uninvited into Clay Horey's house, "seduces his Negro cook, shoots her husband, and finally wins Clay's wife in a crooked crap game, along with his car and his farm." These are not typical results of a pastoral visitation, even in the South.

In another Caldwell work, *A Place Called Estherville,* a virtuous Negro boy, after successfully attempting to preserve his chastity "from the wily seductions of a beautiful, rich, white girl," falls prey to "a sultry white widow who tackles him and rapes him while he is making his deliveries on his bicycle." Negro boys are not all that popular in Southern society.

Faulkner's novels do not reach nearly as many people as Caldwell's, but they win critics and influence people in the upper intellectual brackets. The high praise which critics and the intelligentsia accord them is fairly won. He is one of the most effective narrative writers this country has ever produced.

Honest Southern readers would have to admit that his pictures of life in the South are accurate in minutest detail. Anyone who has ever been in the store of what is known in the South as a "supply man" knows that Faulkner wrote photographically when he noted that his character's books recorded "that slow trickle of molasses and meal and meat, of shoes and straw hats and overalls, of plowlines and collars and heelbolts and clevises, which returned each fall as cotton."

Furthermore, Faulkner knows his people, and he gets the three main classes—the aristocrats, the up-and-coming former poor whites and the Negroes—into his books with amazing success. He knows and tells how they look, think, talk and feel. He sees them with clarity, humor and compassion, and, like any genuine artist, he searches for the truth behind them and the land they live in.

It is, of course, his privilege and business as a novelist to specialize in matricide, patricide, infanticide, incest, rape and plain and fancy murder for the same reason that Aeschylus and Sophocles did. These crimes make good copy. They provide plot fables evocative of "pity and terror." They supply levers for prying into human nature. But Faulkner's fables are no more representations of Mississippi than the *House of Atreus* trilogy and *Oedipus Rex* were accounts of typical days in the life of the ancient Greeks.

There is irony in the fact that, as America gives full "faith and credit" to what Southern novelists say about the South, so the rest of the world gives similar credit to what American novelists say about America. On this very point Perry Miller, professor of American literature at Harvard, who had been lecturing on his subject in Europe wrote in *Harper's Magazine:* "The names are always Lewis, Dos Passos, Hemingway, Faulkner, Steinbeck, Caldwell, Farrell. There are also copies of James M. Cain and of others whom Edmund Wilson dubbed 'the boys in the backroom,' but seldom any representation of those I would call our 'realists.' "

Therefore, said Professor Miller, his European students "asked the question, not idly but anxiously: These writings, they would say, are all vehement attacks on the American way of life; if we are not to take them as meaning that American civilization is a foretaste of hell, how are we to take them?"

The answer is, "With a mountain of salt." It may be asserted with some show of reason that America is not populated exclusively by women dying of boredom in small towns, millionaire gangsters dying at the hands of other millionaire gangsters, by boy friends who murder girl friends, or by starving Oakies and assorted idiots.

A fairly typical representation of the South in modern fiction would run somewhat as follows:

### A Scythe For Mother

Maj. Earl Barringer on his return home from the First World War suspects his bride Camilla (supposedly descended from the fine old Montrose family who moved from Virginia

to the Deep South after the death of old Colonel Barringer—
not the *first* Colonel Barringer but the one before him—
commonly referred to in genealogical records as "Minus
One") of being unfaithful to him with her mulatto half-
brothers Simeon and Samuel. Earl has, in fact, been rather
suspicious of her since learning that she spent her teens in a
sporting house in Natchez-Under-The-Hill.

Awakening early after a fitful sleep on his first night home,
Earl gazes at the pure and placid countenance of his fiery-
haired Camilla on the lace pillow slip in the ancestral
four-poster, until he can stand it no longer.

Jumping from bed and grabbing a scythe, which he habitually kept beside the bedside table for purely personal reasons,
he strides across the dewy grass to Simeon's and Samuel's
cabin, neatly beheads them and sews each one's head to the
other's body to make identification more difficult. With a
giant's strength he carries their bodies on his shoulders to
the decaying mansion where he dumps them in a large vat
of maturing moonshine in an abandoned snake pit under the
front porch.

Next day he places the corpses in the old four-poster, sep-
arating them by a bolster because the bed had a tendency to
sag in the middle.

Camilla comes home the next day from a business trip to
Natchez-Under-The-Hill, drinks a few gourdfuls of the white
lightning from the vat, and goes to bed in place of the bolster
between Sim and Sam without thinking twice about it. But
soon her confusion is pitiable. Earl, who has been watching
the proceedings through the closet keyhole, rushes out in-
tending to kill her in a jealous rage, but chivalrously changes
his mind and hands her the scythe instead, begging her to
kill him.

Always obliging, Camilla separates him at the neck, leaves

his body on the floor, kicks his head under the bed, and goes to sleep.

She has been asleep only a couple of days when her son (by a former friend) Ramon who had just failed his mid-term examinations at Harvard Law School (where he had been sent by Camilla to wean him away from Darling Jean Jitters, the albino daughter of a tenant on the place who was not a fit character for Ramon to associate with) rushes into the room.

More intoxicated than a Southern gentleman should be (because he had generously sampled the moonshine in the vat, which seemed to him to have a better color and bead than ever before) and seeing his mother (of whom he was, alas! too, too fond) in bed between two dark men (who were after all his half-uncles) and also his father's decapitated body on the floor, he requests an explanation.

Camilla jumps from bed in a state of nature (nothing unusual with her), clasps her son to her bosom and tells him he is the only man she ever really loved.

Strangely revolted by all this (a clear victory for Harvard over heredity), Ramon cuts off his mother's head as she kneels in supplication before him. He does it with the scythe. Pitching her body on the bed and jumping in after it, he lights a Murad and burns up the whole shebang.

### Keep Looking

But, you say, somebody must have told the truth about the South. Yes, two classes of writers have—the humorists and the regional analysts. But the first were not believed and the second were not read.

Mark Twain, Augustus Baldwin Longstreet and others succeeded in getting fairly realistic pictures of the South on the printed page—Twain went so far as to locate a one-horse farm in the ante-bellum Southland—but Southerners refused to take them seriously by the simple expedient of cataloguing them as humorists or, worse, as newspaper funny men whose products were used mainly for lining pantry shelves in dark rooms or lighting clay pipes.

The regional analysts—if that is the word for the group of writers which includes Howard W. Odum, author of *Southern Regions,* Rupert B. Vance, author of *The Human Geography of the South,* V. O. Key, author of *Southern Politics,* and Calvin B. Hoover and B. U. Ratchford, authors of *Economic Resources and Policies of the South*—have drawn at least an accurate, comprehensive and detailed diagram, if not portrait, of the South as it is for the god of things as they are.

But he is not our god. So who reads these writers? Their ponderous and illuminating volumes are not sold over the drugstore counter with the morning pack of cigarettes, the midday cheese sandwich and the afternoon coke. Their sales are numbered in the thousands while Caldwell's are numbered in the millions.

From which source, then, does the great American public derive its quaint and curious notions about the South? There can be no doubt. Truth, as far as the South is concerned, is more of a stranger than fiction.

Therefore the answer to the question, "Is it true what they say about Dixie?" must be, "No, no, a thousand times no."

The South shrugs it all off by adopting the legend over the fireplace of the late George Bernard Shaw: "They say. What say they? Let them say."

But curiosity, stooping to poke a wetted finger through the paper screen, asks again, "What is the South?"

# 2

## Two Souths Have I—
## And to Both I am True

To begin to understand the South one must know that it is not one but two, that there are two Souths which exist side by side in each Southern state, but are as different as Chicago and Bangkok.

They are called the Old South and the New South, but these names are not accurate.

The Old South of the great mansions and feudal plantations is no more; it died when the Emancipation Proclamation was born. Nevertheless, remnants of the Old South survive here and there from Virginia to Texas. They resemble the Old South as a grandson resembles a grandfather or as "the mist resembles the rain," but they are not the Old South. A better name would be the "Surviving South."

The New South is not altogether new, nor is that name quite right. There is usually something of the "fallen day" of the Old South about it, although not enough, to be sure, to make it feel much out of place if it should be transported by some necromancy to Pennsylvania or New Jersey and dumped down there. The reason is that the New South really is the "Industrialized South."

But nobody is going to call these two Souths the "Surviving South" and the "Industrialized South."

So, now that it is understood what we do not mean by the terms, we can go back to using "Old South" and "New South" with better conscience and more clarity.

The New South, by and large, lives in the hill country where waterpower was found for industry and where slavery never got a foothold. The Old South lives in the coastal plain or tidewater areas where there never has been much industry and where the flood of slavery has left a lot of flotsam and jetsam.

The New South used to live in towns, but now it lives in cities, from Roanoke, Virginia, to Houston, Texas. The Old South, which used to live in the country in great houses with fancy names like "Esmeralda," now is found mainly in a few old, proud and scattered towns.

The Old South grows raw materials, such as cotton, tobacco, rice, corn and peanuts. The New South produces manufactured goods, such as textiles, cigarettes, furniture, radios, television sets and atomic bombs.

The New South works hard—probably harder in terms of foot-pounds per capita than New York, Chicago or Pittsburgh. The Old South takes it easy. The New South emulates the ant; the Old South considers the lilies of the field. The New South would rather play golf or tennis; the Old South would rather go fishing.

The New South makes "good money," as it calls it—a phrase at which the Old South sniffs audibly. The New South has a deep respect for money; it judges people by the amount they make and the part of town they live in, which comes to the same thing because when a man makes enough money his wife moves him and the family into a new, fresh and pretty suburban development with a dolled-up name, such as "Stardust Park," where they proudly build or buy a house next door to neighbors in their income-tax bracket and unconsciously agree with the man who said, "The joy of life is in the steep ascent and looking down on those who once looked down on you." A woman living in Stardust Park will say to one who lived there once but who has moved back into town—a matter of a couple of miles—"We intended to call on you but were so sorry we didn't get to see you all before you left," so that one is tempted to ask her if she couldn't send a postcard saying, "Having wonderful time—wish you were here!" There are no angels with flaming swords guarding the entrance to Stardust Park, but this seems to be an oversight on the part of Providence which will be rectified in time by the Real Estate Board.

## Planned Inactivity

The Old South does not despise money, although it is somewhat suspicious of it, except in the largest amounts, in which case *fides omnia vincit*. It will accept any given amount graciously as something which it has somehow mislaid for a season, but it will not overexercise itself to acquire it.

The New South is always building or buying houses. A member of the Old South does not build a house because he was born with one, and he does not buy one for the same reason the patrician lady of Boston doesn't buy a hat—she already has one.

The old South has a code which includes courage, integrity and compassion; it is not much affected by money or anything else. It is not as old as the laws of the Medes or as wide as the code of Hammurabi, but 'tis enough, 'twill serve.

It is the one handed down by the Southern fathers and where it still exists it works.

The Old South does not ask what a man has, and it can get along without knowing what he does, if anything. It *would like* to know who his folks are. But it *has* to know whether he is amusing.

Laurence Stallings once said that what he liked about Charleston was that it had "resisted Abraham Lincoln's attempts to put the country into Arrow collars." Honest Abe may sound a bit misplaced in the role of the Arrow collar man, but it is true that the Old South, while it wears the things on occasion, is not exactly collar conscious.

In fact, the Old South is a place where a man will go around with a hole in his sock, or for that matter in his breeches, and feel no more embarrassed by it than a king would be. A hole, he assures himself, is something that might happen to anybody any time, but a darn or a patch in a garment smacks of an attempt to make your poverty, or at any rate your wife's industriousness, conspicuous and thus evinces a low-bred sensitiveness to public opinion.

The New South, like Martha, is careful about many things. The Old South just doesn't give a damn. It did its worrying fourscore years ago, and it has about worried out.

The New South is determined to have its daughter "come out" at the annual debutante ball, and will go to great lengths and expense to get her "out." The Old South reasons that, if its daughter isn't invited (and often she is not), that merely goes to show that the debutante ball is not so much a social occasion as it is a roundup of the new-rich herd by the hucksters.

The New South is energetic. The Old South has no intention of scurrying to reach the "point of no return." It prefers to exercise what John C. Calhoun called "a wise and masterly inactivity." What a wonderful phrase! No one but a true Southerner of the old school could possibly have invented it. Many Southerners throughout history have adopted it unconsciously and instinctively as a program. What they practiced often wasn't wise, and it was rarely masterly, but it certainly was inactivity.

### Two Souths—Two Ways of Life

Yes, the two Souths which live side by side have very different ways of life. The New South is symbolized by the H-bomb plant rising in the Savannah River basin between Aiken, South Carolina and Augusta, Georgia. The Old South is symbolized by a double-barreled cannon on the courthouse square in Athens, Georgia, which couldn't hit a forest. The cannon was invented during the Civil War and the inventor's idea was that two cannon balls connected by a chain would emerge simultaneously from the twin barrels horizontally aligned and mow down the ranks of the enemy. But when the Confederates tested it by aiming it at a forest, one ball came out before the other and the chain made them act like a boomerang. Anyway, the charge missed the whole forest and the Confederate Army scrapped its secret weapon. Still, it was quite an idea.

The Old South is the magnificent Capitol of the Confederacy on Goat Hill in Montgomery, Alabama. It is also the White House of the Confederacy nearby, which contains a picture showing that the South won The War. From the picture it is patent that General Grant is surrendering to General Lee. Grant is disheveled, stooped-over, crestfallen, hopeless. Lee is immaculate, erect, confident, triumphant.

The New South is Birmingham, Alabama, which wasn't even born until the Civil War was over. It is a city built by steel, and the profits are flowering in medical research, an art gallery, a symphony orchestra and homes that look like palaces.

The Old South is Columbia, South Carolina, with its beautiful classic capitol designed by the great Robert Mills of Charleston, still pockmarked by Sherman's cannon and surmounted by a dinky dome which somebody stuck on it after the architect's death. In front of the capitol is Houdon's statue of George Washington with a broken cane. Old-timers in Columbia will tell you that Yankee troops broke the cane under the impression that Washington was Jeff Davis. They have no intention of repairing it.

The New South is Asheville, North Carolina, with its Ecusta cigarette paper factory and its Oerlikon precision instruments and arms plant.

The Old South is of course "old Charleston," where the few favored sons who have a house on the Batt'ry, a plantation in the hinterland and a cottage on the Isle of Palms don't believe in change. Why should they? Naturally they didn't like Truman or Roosevelt, and naturally they think the Civil War turned out wrong, but they aren't at all sure that the American Revolution turned out right. "You know," one of them will tell you, "South Carolina got Virginia in the war between the states in revenge for Virginia's getting South Carolina in the Revolution."

The New South is Houston, Texas, with its "five hundred poor and rich millionaires."

The Old South is the old hotel in Montgomery, Alabama, where Sidney Lanier once clerked—a far cry from "The Marshes of Glynn." The Old South is Stone Mountain, that dark gray mound which resembles a petrified whale emerging from the earth, with profiles of Jefferson Davis, Lee and Jackson visible, like a triple Jonah, in the belly of the monster.

The New South is Du Pont's huge nylon plant in Martins-ville, Virginia.

The Old South is Rhett Butler remarking in *Gone With the Wind,* that the South was the only country in modern history that ever started a war without having a single can-non factory.

Thus the South today is a marvelous mixture of romance and business, history and hurry, magnolias and steel mills, azaleas and acrilan, heaven and hell-bombs.

### The Country and the People

The South is my country, and its people are my peo-ple.

The country stretches crescentwise from the honey-colored sand dunes of the Virginia and Carolina coasts to the sandy wastes of Texas which are bright enough on a moonlit night to let a soldier read a love letter.

Some of the land is skeleton-poor, worn out and aban-doned to gullies, broomstraw and scrub oaks. Some is treach-erous swamp land, infested with strange "varmints" and going by such awesome names as the Great Dismal and Oke-fenokee. Some is deep, rich, invincibly fertile coastal plain, valley or delta land, sprouting fabulous crops of cotton, corn, sugar cane, rice and a thousand other commodities.

Some of it is foothill land, surging in vast waves of green from the coastal plains to the mountains. This is the land of which Bishop Spangenberg wrote in 1753: "It is the middle of the winter and the ground is covered with snow, but we are camping in the forest, well and content under the wings of the Almighty."

Some of it is mountain land of rugged ridges and deep gorges with Indian names like Nantahala and Cullasaja, a

land tilted skyward and taking all shapes from domes to pin-
nacles. These mountains are never barren but are always
verdant; summer touches them with purple rhododendrons
and flame azaleas; autumn turns them into vistas of color
which look like rainbows that have been run through sausage
grinders or cathedral windows which have been bombed and
swept together again.

The mountains and the great meadows beyond them called
irresistibly to the hunters and pioneers who fell in love with
a lovely, beckoning land, and left everything for it. Undergoing all hardships and perils, they accounted themselves a
"happy breed of men." Daniel Boone, coming back miraculously alive from his odyssey on the buffalo trails and in the
laurel thickets and the rhododendron hells, where no white
had ever been before, told the stockade stay-at-homes: "I
never felt lost the whole enduring time." The mountains
and the valleys were like the form of a beloved but cruel
mistress whom the pioneers were determined to possess or
die; many did both.

Even today the South has a variegated beauty which is apt
to charm the beholder. Raymond Mortimer expressed something of its fascination in the London *Times:*

The more I saw of the South, the better I liked it. The creeks
in Louisiana, with drifting islands of flowers and cypress draped
with long veils of Spanish moss; the red earth of Georgia and the
Carolinas; the vast Tennessee River, subjugated by monumental
dams among lushly wooded hills; the colonnaded plantation
houses with their avenues of oaks or magnolias above the levees
of the Mississippi; the campus of the University of Virginia,
designed by Jefferson, as happy and complete an architectural
composition as anything that Europe can show; the velvety, volup-
tuous night-sky and the leisurely pace of daily life; all these
predispose to sympathy.

Our place names betray us; they are witnesses of what we loved or feared or what we considered beautiful, dangerous or funny; they are the tablets of our memory.

There are Indian names such as Roanoke, Shenandoah, Hatteras, Chincoteague, Tuscaloosa, Talapoosa, Chickasaw, Choctaw, Cherokee, Chattaloochie, Okechobee, Osceola, Watauga, Cullowhee, Currituck, Manteo, Ocracoke, Alabama, Tennessee, Mississippi, Arkansas, Kentucky, Texas—and even more outlandish names like Catahoula, Yalobushee, Itawamba, Shuqualak and Ogeechee.

There are names which go far back in English or European history, such as Sussex, Norfolk, Suffolk, Cumberland, Southampton, Halifax, Amherst, Princess Anne, William and Mary, Cartaret, Granville, Hyde, Raleigh, Airlie, Iberville, La Salle, Baton Rouge, Virginia, Carolina, Georgia and Louisiana.

There are classical names like Rome, Troy, Carthage, Sparta, Athens, Sabine, Agricola.

There are names chosen for their beauty, such as Savannah, Florida, Vermilion, Bellefontaine, Sapphire, Marigold, Plumtree, Rodanthe, Sweetwater, Jewel Ridge, Whiteapple, Azalea and Evangeline.

There are names picked to commemorate battles, the Bible and famous men, such as Shiloh, Bethel, Buena Vista, Washington, Jefferson, Lee, Jackson, Oglethorpe, Randolph, Macon, Lafayette, Meriwether.

There are queer names which set one wondering, such as Smoky Ordinary, Vinegar Bend, Moccasin Gap, Ripshin Ridge, Paint Gap, Possum Quarter, Lickskillet, Stinking Gut, Nags Head, Kill Devil Hill, Banner Elk, Whalebone Inlet, Society Hill, Due West, Honea Path, Turn Out, Cross Anchor, Nine Times, Nowhere Branch, Fair Play, Nobottom Creek, Beargrass, Lost Cove, Caesar's Head, Pigeon Forge, Cape Fear and Cat Hollow.

## Our People

Our people are, in the main, the descendants of those who conquered, or were conquered by, the land a couple of centuries or so ago. Our four principal divisions are: The Anglo-Saxons, the Scotch-Irish, the Germans and the Negroes. Since our population has grown in that time almost entirely by natural increase rather than by immigration, the ratios of our racial strains are pretty much what they were in the late 1700's.

There is a sprinkling of French, Spanish, Mexicans and other breeds on the fringes of the South, but most Southerners look on these people as fleeting and exotic visitors, regardless of how many hundreds of years they have been here.

The qualities of the big-four racial strains in the South have remained fairly constant, too. The Anglo-Saxons were, and are, a law-making and law-breaking people, commercial-minded, rather poor at farming, courageous, somewhat insensitive, and possessed of the determination of the devil. In brief, they exhibited the cardinal qualities needed to build a civilization in the wilderness.

The Scotch-Irish (called pure Scotch by historians who contend that the Scots never intermingled with the Irish during their sojourn in Ireland, which goes to show how little historians know about such matters) emigrated first to Pennsylvania and other Northern states, then drove themselves westward until they ran into the Appalachian Mountains, whence they slid southwestwardly into Virginia, North Carolina, South Carolina and Georgia. They were, and are, fiery, proud, imaginative, bold, stoical, democratic; lovers of religion, learning, liberty and statecraft; their heroes are the preacher, the teacher and the statesman, and they have produced them wholesale.

The Germans were practical, economical, hard-working and good-natured; they were mainly farmers and businessmen, placing much stress on school, church and store, but little on politics.

The Negro was the hewer of wood and the picker of cotton, the lover of laughter and song, the one who worked and loafed most, enjoyed most and endured most—a people constructed of unsurpassed material for absorbing the shocks of life as a rubber tire absorbs the shocks of the road.

Our people have been subjected to more than ordinary trials and tribulations. We live in a lush, lotus-eating land where the temptations of the flesh, including gluttony, lust and anger, need strong curbs if we are to overcome them. Therefore, we must have a standard and abide by it. To exist we must resist. We do not all have the same standard. Some of us have a moral and religious standard which makes us puritanical as Cotton Mather and more stoical than Seneca. Others of us have a standard which we call a code of honor and which allows for a large measure of epicureanism but which has boundaries as definite as an electric fence. Some kick over all standards and codes, go native and wallow in the mire of Tobacco Road.

We have learned that the family is the most effective instrument for keeping individuals up to a standard. This helps explain the extreme clannishness of the South. On the other hand it helps explain our individualism; the family would be too boring to exist if all the kinfolks were too much alike.

As Southerners we have known nature and civilization, victory and defeat, wealth and poverty. We are not always as simple as we look and hardly ever as simple as we talk.

# 3

## Picture Window — Southern Exposure

Let us look at the Old South the only way we can look at it, by visiting one of the small towns where it still lives. Let us go to Hastings. Let us look at it with some care, because there is something fine (exasperating, too) about it, and because it may not be with us long. Like the bison, the carrier pigeon and the daguerreotype of great-great grandfather, it is fading away—fading away with the homes, characters, culture, customs and code which made it what it was.

Hastings is not a typical town of the Old South, because there is no such thing. The rest of the country may run to types and standards all it wants to, but the Old South runs to individuals and characters. Hastings is a symbol.

Nothing lives forever, and so the little towns where the Old South still resides either grow into cities and become the New South, or the people who make them what they are die or move away to the cities to earn a living. A few, a very few, cities—Charleston, New Orleans, Natchez, Richmond, in spots—by contrariness of character keep something of the

Old South about them, as Boston, at least on Beacon Hill, keeps something of the granite-like Emersonian imprint of the Old New England about it. But you can count these cities on the fingers of one hand, because the Old South, which survived the move from plantations to towns smaller than plantations nearly a century ago, can only in rare instances acclimatize itself to the standardization, smog, traffic and tempo of urban life.

So by all means let us go to Hastings, even if it takes some time and trouble, as it will because Hastings is on no railroad (a choice it made more than a century ago) or main traveled highway or airline. Let us drop in on the center of town, the courthouse square with its English elms and buttercups. From the courthouse portico, between the two middle columns, George Washington addressed the citizens of Hastings on his Southern tour in the late 1700's and made private entry in his journal which indicated that he was "sorry to see that Hastings is not keeping up with the march of progress." Old Miss Anabel Carewe, descendant of Col. Richard Carewe who introduced the distinguished visitor on that occasion, has a letter from General Washington in the rosewood desk in the parlor of her home a couple of blocks from the square, but refuses to keep it in a safe because it is "only a bread-and-butter letter."

Col. Aaron Burr rested momentarily under the shade of the trees on the courthouse lawn when they took him to Richmond to be tried before the great Chief Justice Marshall, and the people of Hastings had considerable sympathy for the colonel, partly because he had "such nice manners," and partly because his talented daughter Theodosia had married an Allston, even if he was one of the South Carolina Allstons rather than one of the Hastings Alstons.

On the old records in the office of the Clerk of the Court in Hastings is this entry:

| *Date* | *Name* | *Charge* | *Verdict* |
|--------|--------|----------|-----------|
| June 20 | Mrs. Catherine Ethridge | Murder | Not Guilty |

Hastings can fill in the details with the aid of tradition. Catherine Ethridge was the mother of Judge James Ethridge, General Ethan Ethridge and Governor Harold Ethridge. Furthermore, she was a woman of unusual beauty, courage and character. A white man named Jack Weeks had become infatuated with her slave girl Alice and had been attempting to visit her at night in her house in the Ethridge back yard. Alice and her husband both appealed to Mrs. Ethridge to keep him away.

Mrs. Ethridge ordered Weeks not to come on her premises. He persisted. She then warned him that if she caught him there again she would kill him.

Not long afterwards Weeks was found one morning shot to death in the Ethridge back yard. It had snowed during the night and a woman's tracks led from the body to the Ethridge home. Catherine Ethridge was indicted for murder in the first degree and placed in jail.

Robert Jones, later attorney general of the Confederacy, was her lawyer. At the trial he did not cross-examine any state's witness, put on any evidence for his client, or allow her to testify in her behalf, although the state had made out what appeared to be an airtight case.

Not having introduced any evidence, Mr. Jones had the concluding speech to the jury. This consisted of only twelve words. He merely asked his lovely client to stand directly in front of the jury. Then he said, "Gentlemen, could so beautiful a creature have committed so foul a crime?"

The jury, as one man, said, "No."

Time in Hastings is not a swiftly moving point but a panorama full of color and drama stretching back a long way. Time is something which the people trust and savor as

it comes to them, but few have quite the perfect confidence
in it that Lawyer Purefoy had when he wrote in his will, duly
recorded in the Clerk's office: "I give and bequeath to my
son William my slave girl Venus, to have and enjoy her
forever."

In the heart of town stands the courthouse, which plays a
major role in the affairs of all citizens. Entering it is an
ancient Negro man, one without guile, who is after an old-
age pension. He goes into the Welfare Office and makes
known his want to Miss Lucy Abbott, the welfare officer.
She can tell by looking at him that he is nearer one hundred
than sixty-five, but she also knows that the government does
not go by looks in such matters. So she asks, "Do you know
how old you are, Uncle Gabe?" but without any real hope
that he does.

"Yes, ma'm."

"I don't mean *about* how old," she says, "I have to know
*exactly*. Can you tell me the year and month and day you
were born?"

"Yes, ma'm."

"Well, when was it?"

"Hit was," says Uncle Gabe triumphantly, "the first clear
Sunday after General Lee surrendered."

Hastings is situated on a slight ridge of land which must
have been originally covered with an oak forest; some of the
oaks are still standing, very big and centuries old. Hastings'
Main Street, which incidentally is no kin to Sinclair Lewis'
Main Street, runs north and south and is a pleasant thorough-
fare, not because of its stores and buildings which often resemble a "beggarly collection of empty boxes," but because
of its trees. In addition to the oaks there are mulberries and
English elms. Nobody knows who planted the mulberries or
why (unless it was some crank who expected to make silk),
but everybody knows who planted the elms whose branches

now meet over the street. It was General Thomas Jefferson
Grayson (the one who went out to Texas, planting legisla-
tures and elms on his way) and the elms will flourish in
Hastings' business district as long as there is a lineal descendant of General Grayson to shoulder a shotgun and prevent
the street committee from cutting them down and filling the
stump holes with concrete.

In Fairview cemetery, just west of town, is a monument to
General Grayson (who finally could and did come home
again) with his exploits carved on it. When a life of General
Sam Houston was published some years ago, the people of
Hastings, knowing that Houston and Grayson had fought together for Texan independence, read it avidly in expectation
that General Houston would have something nice to say
about General Grayson, but they were shocked to find that
all General Houston said was, "General Grayson has all the
qualities of a dog except that of faithfulness." Evidently
they *had* fought together. What General Grayson said of
General Houston was not recorded, there being no asbestos
paper handy.

The Episcopal church stands where the business section
shades off into the residential section of Hastings. It is an
old brick building which was paid for in English pounds
about 1800. In front of it is a historical marker noting the
fact that shortly before the Civil War Horace Greeley was
married there to a Miss Mary Cheney who had come South as
a sort of educational missionary to the Negroes.

Inside the church hanging on the wall is a large painting
of a madonna and child which was given by the Pope of
Rome in the old days to Bishop Havergal when he made his
European tour and temporarily joined the Catholic Church.
When he got back home he gave the painting to his old
Episcopal church, and the people of Hastings, although they

were a little suspicious of the painting, saw no sense in letting it go to waste.

Stained glass windows depicting Biblical scenes adorn the church walls; most of them were given in memory of departed parishioners long ago. One shows Christ as a child in His father's carpentry shop; another shows Him, surrounded by children, saying, "Suffer little children to come unto me . . . for of such is the kingdom of heaven." The parents of Hastings took this literally, for they rarely punished a child, anticipating modern progressive education by many years, but were generally content to risk loving him into a state of civilization, and strange to say, it frequently worked, given sufficient time and tribulation. Another window shows Christ as the Good Shepherd, and still another shows the crucifixion with the inscription, "I am the Resurrection and the Life." But the window which the people of Hastings like best is the one which pictures Christ with his arms outstretched saying, "Come unto me all ye that labor and are heavy laden, and I will give you rest." They may not have labored much, but they have been heavy laden.

It was doubtless these windows with their rich yet mellow coloring that moved Jim West, the old Negro poet of Hastings, to write:

> There is six churches in this town,
> And the Methodist church makes seven;
> The Episcopal church sets in the middle
> And the insides look like heaven.

The old church, with its gallery for its colored communicants, has seen its share of joy and sorrow—which became, not merely individual but congregational, and even community, joys and sorrows—with the church heightening the joy and softening the sorrow in christenings, marriages and funerals.

Not far from the church is the brick house surrounded by

the picket fence where Great-aunt Evelina used to live.
Uncle Colin, her brother, was the one who in the old days
courted one of two sisters, but got their names confused and
proposed by letter to the wrong one. She accepted him by
return mail and he was too much of a gentleman to let her
know of his mistake.

Aunt Lina, however, did inform her, and Uncle Colin
lived a bachelor the rest of his life (he didn't propose to get
into any more romantic mazes) in Aunt Lina's home reading
French novels, which was considered a dangerous and per-
verse practice in those days.

There was one other thing that Uncle Colin was noted for.
In the desperately poverty-stricken days of the Reconstruction Era his brother Ben, who had gone to New York and
become head of the Cotton Exchange, and incidentally become very advanced in his views, sent Brother Colin a subscription to the New York *Tribune*. After reading one issue
Colin canceled his subscription with a few well-heated words
and sent a copy of his letter—copied by hand, of course—to
Brother Ben. Ben, still determined to do something handsome for his brother, sent Colin a twenty-dollar bill by
registered mail. Colin could not use it, because nobody in
Hastings could change it during that era, but it was a source
of credit and gave him the reputation of being a capitalist,
which lasted the rest of his life.

When the big North-South railroad came through this section of the state back in the old days, the people of Hastings
wouldn't let it come through their town, which happened to
be on the direct line, so the railroad made a detour around
it, missing it by three miles. The people had various reasons
for not wanting the railroad: it would scare the horses, cows
and chickens; it would be a fire hazard, not to mention a
smoke and noise nuisance, and it would bring undesirable
characters into town.

But when they saw that the towns on the line were pros-
pering they decided to build a railroad of their own to con-
nect with the main line, for the shipment of goods and the
conveyance of passengers. So the Hastings Railroad came
into being. Its first conductor, Captain C. T. Longstreet,
commemorated the event with verses which started off as
follows:

> In 1886
> With effort duly crowned
> A railroad bed they did affix
> From the S. A. L. to town.

Being a railroad man in those days was something like
being a television actor or a professional baseball player today. Railroad men were a guild of privileged spirits who
looked down on any other mode of transportation. Captain
Longstreet reflected this view when he wrote:

> The Good Book says you shall not covet
> Your neighbor's ox nor his ass,
> But a being of any sanity
> Would let such creatures pass.

Captain Longstreet was an imposing figure of a man as he
stood on the back platform of his train composing poetry
while the wind blew his long white beard over his shoulder,
disclosing the brass buttons on his blue vest. He composed
poetry only every other year. These were the odd (not even)
years when his train backed into Hastings and he could get
the full effect of the view and the breeze. If this is not quite
clear, it should be understood that the Hastings train could
not turn around on its own track. One year it went forward
to the main line and "backed back" (as the folks said) into
Hastings. The next year it reversed the process, after visiting
the roundhouse on the main line, but Captain Longstreet
could find no inspiration while backing into the main line.

He could woo the muse only while backing into Hastings.

It has always been a very informal railroad, since it was owned not by a soulless corporation but by the townspeople themselves. But in the old days it was even more informal than it is now. The train, which generally consisted of an engine, a boxcar and a passenger car, would stop at any place to pick up a passenger, provided Captain Longstreet recognized him and was not mad with him at the time. Kids hopped rides on it when nobody was looking and placed crossed pins on the track in front of it which were magically transformed into scissors after the wheels had run over them. Quite a few kids used to play train in the engine on Sundays, twisting every knob and pulling every lever they saw. Every Sunday, that is, when Alpheus Conover, who was town clerk, wasn't using it. Alpheus used to cut wood for the engine on Fridays and Saturdays for the privilege of taking his young lady, Louise, to ride in it on Sundays. It was quite a privilege, too, in the pre-automobile days when "the Dummy," as the engine was affectionately known, was the fastest thing on wheels. Louise couldn't resist such romantic and adventurous wooing; she married Alpheus after the seventh ride.

During the First World War, the United States Government, after some trouble with strikes, decided that it had to run all the railroads in the country, but the news hadn't reached Hastings (or at any rate hadn't made any impression on it) when one day an army captain walked into the depot, where the superintendent and the engineer were engaged in a hot checker game (with the fireman kibitzing) between trains, and informed his astounded listeners that he had come to take over their railroad. They protested rather violently and profanely at first, but when he explained the situation to them they acquiesced but told him he had better take a hand at a checker game since it was a longer time between trains than drinks. He did, and for the duration the United States ran the Hastings Railroad between checker games.

Miss Laura Hastings once wrote "A History of Hastings" in which she referred to certain of the inhabitants as "good, substantial citizens." Nothing could have insulted them more. That phrase took away their individuality and demoted them from "characters" to people. It put them outside the class of old Judge Alfred Crabtree who hated so many people that he couldn't keep them straight and so he used to sit on his porch and ask his wife, "What am I mad at that damned scoundrel for, Marina?" as his foes passed by, or Charlie Taliaferro who was so conceited that it got to be a common saying that "God Almighty's overcoat wouldn't make Charlie a vest."

And then there is "Cousin" Emily Marshall who lives in the old Marshall place with all the boxwood planted in the shape of hearts and diamonds, and with the schoolhouse in the yard.

She is "around" ninety years old and has been teaching in Hastings for nearly three-quarters of a century. All call her "Cousin Emily," and in reality three generations of the people of Hastings are "her children" by right of teachership. She has no use for the public schools and she never heard of progressive education or John Dewey, although she prides herself on using the "most modern"—by which she means "the Montessori"—method. In fact, her method is all love and pride and patience. Her books are the *McGuffey Readers*, Webster's *Blue Back Speller*, and *Fifty Famous Stories* which go back to Plutarch.

No pupil of hers ever gets out of a book without knowing it page by page and word by word, but as soon as he achieves that he gets out of it then and there. Every Christmas and May she gives to her prize pupils cards that look like valentines with the words, "For Excellence in Spelling" inscribed

on them in her bold but shaky handwriting. Her pupils may
not learn much about many things but they learn to value
the brightness that will cling to that almost forgotten word
"excellence" all their lives, and they learn to catch hold of a
tradition stretching without a break far, far back from a small
town of the Old South to London and Rome and Athens and
Jerusalem.

When she reads this book she will be proud of it in front
of others because one of her "children" wrote it, but to me
she will say gently regarding the shoddy passages, "William, I
don't think you did your best there," and I will know that
she is right.

### Spring in Hastings

Spring comes to us in Hastings when maples redden, cherry
trees whiten, willows clothe themselves in diaphanous green
and violets peep through the grass. This is the season of the
yellow jasmine, the red japonica and the flowering bush we
call "first-breath-of-spring" which fills the air with the clean-
est, sweetest perfume in the world. Spring comes through in
emerald lakes of wheat and rye, in yellow pools of mustard
and turnip "salat," and in little fountains of white spiraea
and golden forsythia.

Pear, peach, cherry and plum blossoms are pink and white
against the ash-gray weatherboarding of old houses, none of
which is so poverty-stricken or tumble-down but that it has
its flowering fruit tree.

Spring comes suddenly in this part of the country. One
day there will be a mist of Judas trees on the hillside, so dim
and delicate against gray boughs and green pines that it is
hard to say whether it is pink or purple or lavender; it is a
blossoming that comes before the dogwood dares and takes
the winds of March with beauty. Then all at once it is gone
before we have even bothered to give it a decent name.

But in some years the redbud waits on the edge of the forest for the white surf of the dogwood to overtake it and that combination makes a spring worth remembering.

Broomstraw tawny as a lion's mane glows against the olive-green of old-field pines; jonquils light their little lamps; lilacs, wisteria and azaleas join the crowd; bees visit the iris; white butterflies try their wings in the blue air; boys get out their fishing poles and baseball bats. It is the season of "the apple tree, the singing and the gold . . . all life that is wild and young." Shakespeare is its poet and Mozart its musician. Spring's gold is not weighed; its beauty is that of youth—innocent, importunate, improvident and bittersweet.

## Small Town, Spring Night

Main Street in Hastings is crowded because it is Saturday night, and people have come in from the countryside, some to buy their rations for the week and others just for the romance and excitement of the thing.

The electric sign in front of the drugstore glows red and green against an ink-blue sky while a man fascinated by it stumps his toe on pavement broken by maple roots. A young fellow in a stripped-down model-T Ford with an illuminated kewpie doll for a radiator cap hollers, "Hello, heathen!" to a buxom, black-haired girl in a pink rayon dress. High-pitched laughter fills the soft air. Old friends greet one another with, "What's the good word?" A baby, parked in the front seat of a truck, waves its arms and legs like a capsized beetle. Weary Negroes sit on the tops of garbage cans, fanning their patient faces with their hats.

The popcorn and hot-dog man confides to a friend, "I have to know all the wrinkles in this trade. I make folks eat with me instead of going home to supper. When a hungry man passes by, I fan the smell his way. He says, 'What's dat I

smell?' I say, 'Dat's a hot dog.' He says, 'Gimme one.' I
tell him, 'Eat five and I'll give you a shamrock free.' My best
dogs are shamrocks. He'll buy five then and eat six, and I've
got me a customer for life. I don't make much money, but
I get a lot of fun out of selling 'em. My wife thinks I'm the
best man in the world. Sometimes I bring her a present like
I do the children. I'm taking her this apple tonight. I know
I'm going to spoil her, but I love her so much I just can't
help it."

Next door to the drugstore is Lawyer Horace Eaton's
office, the brick building with the little rose garden in front.
The office is lighted up tonight because Lawyer Eaton is
playing poker with a bunch of the boys in the back room.
He is a "character"; he can do and say what he pleases, since
he has long ago given up his political ambitions; he has the
works of Ingersoll and Maupassant on his shelves next to
Blackstone and *Corpus Juris;* he is as much a poet and actor
as a lawyer; he does not go to church but he knows more
about the Bible than those who do; he lives by a code which
he sums up in Robert Burns' injunction, "But where you
feel your honor grip, let that aye be your border." He has
never been to college, having been too poor to pay and too
proud to work his way through, but he has lent or given
money to a dozen boys and girls to send them to the state
university; he tells them, "Read the Bible, Shakespeare,
Plato and Macaulay." The poor whites and Negroes come
to him to do their "lawing" for them: they know by experience that he will usually get them out of "trouble"; he does
it because he very frequently sees no reason why they should
be punished for breaking a code of law or morals to which
they never subscribed. So they say of him when they run
into difficulties with the law or with their supply man, "It's
Lawyer Eaton for us—or else Lawyer Bushes."

Uncle Wash Williams, the old Negro who is entering Mr.

Eaton's office at this time of night, has gotten in trouble with his supply man, Mr. Eugene Haithcock, known to Uncle Wash and other Negroes as "Mr. Bluejean." He has threatened to put Uncle Wash on the roads for eating a pig. True, the pig was only a small one. True, it belonged to Uncle Wash. But he has given Mr. Bluejean a mortgage on it, together with his crop, for last year's supplies. True, Uncle Wash has paid the debt. But he has also beyond any reasonable doubt eaten the pig, and so is technically guilty of "disposing of mortgaged property." Why then is Mr. Bluejean threatening Uncle Wash? Because Mr. Bluejean wants Uncle Wash to sell him his homeplace, and Uncle Wash stubbornly refuses to sell it because he knows as well as Mr. Bluejean does that the new, hard-surfaced road is going to run right through it and double its value. He further knows that it is one of Mr. Bluejean's oldest tricks to get a pig in a mortgage, because it gives him a hold on his borrower.

Uncle Wash carefully puts his battered hat in the coal scuttle (all offices have grates for coal fires) and states his case. Lawyer Eaton listens intently. Then he draws a circle on the floor around Wash with a piece of chalk, spits in it, raises his hands to heaven and cries out in mock incantation, "Lord, have mercy on this poor Negro."

Then he pokes his head out of the window and yells, "Gene!" Mr. Haithcock, who has been sitting on a bench in front of the office swapping yarns with a couple of friends, gets up quickly and comes in the office.

"Gene," says Lawyer Eaton, "you can't get Wash's land with that ancient pig trick."

"Why can't I? He's disposed of mortgaged property, hasn't he?"

"Because I'll pick a jury of men you've had dealings with. They'll be onto you, and they'll never convict him. In fact,

I'll have you taxed with the costs for frivolous and malicious prosecution."

Mr. Bluejean thinks this over for a while and then he says, "Well, Mr. Eaton, you couldn't blame me for trying."

"I do blame you. It was a low-down, trifling thing to do."

Wash has sidled to the door. "You can go ahead, Wash," says Mr. Eaton, "I'll hold Mr. Bluejean off you."

"Thank you, sir, thank you, boss," says Wash bowing out. "You may have a white skin, Lawyer Eaton, but you shore has got a black heart."

"I wish you'd let me retain you by the year, Mr. Eaton," says the supply man. "As I've said before, I'd pay you well."

"You know you can't hire me, Gene. What makes you do like you do?"

"I was brought up that way," says the supply man. "My father was a rich man. He died when I was a child and left a big estate to my mother. My uncle got his hands on it and squandered it all. My mother told me about it time and again. Finally the creditors went to law and got out proceedings to sell the last of the land and the personal effects at public auction, including my cradle. Did you ever have your cradle sold out from under you? My mother was a young lady with two small children besides me.

"She went to Exum, the county seat, to get her a lawyer. All of them refused to take the case; they had been retained by the creditors. All, that is, except a drunkard and broken-down aristocrat by the name of John Sharpe Taliaferro. She went to his home—he had long ago given up his office—and a colored cook let her into the parlor where she found Mr. John Sharpe with bottles and books piled up around him every which a-way. He staggered to his feet—he was a wreck, didn't weigh a hundred pounds—and said, 'Madam, state your case.'

"She did and he said, 'Madam, I can save you, if you will

do exactly as I say.' He made out three accounts against the estate for one thousand dollars each. They were bills for services rendered by her in raising me and my two small brothers.

" 'When what is left of the property is put up for auction,' he advised my mother, 'you go to the sale, and when the auctioneer puts up anything for sale, you bid it in.'

" 'But I have no money,' my mother said.

" 'It makes no difference, madam. No one will bid against the widow. You bid it all in for three thousand dollars, and when the administrator comes to collect from you, just present these bills to him.'

"She did exactly what he told her and wound up with the five hundred acres of land, the household furnishings and the cradle.

"From then on she always told us boys that we were very poor, which we were, and that we would never get anything, or make any money or be anybody, except by our wits. So my brother and I got in the habit of sharpening our wits on each other when nobody else was handy. We did a lot of trading and would get the best of anybody, especially each other. And that's why I'm well off today."

"I see," said Mr. Eaton. "But I'll tell you one thing, Gene, you aren't going to get Wash's homeplace."

In the hush of summer twilight, swallows circle the schoolhouse chimney, like skaters in an aerial rink, before darting in, one after another, for the night. Bullbats swoop in unaccountable parabolas and fireflies spangle the valley. There is the muffled sound of chickens settling to roost. Katydids, dryflies and tree toads make a fine rain of shrill sound, as if each leaf and blade of grass had found a tiny voice. Passing lights etch the tropical fronds of heaven trees on white walls, and from a darkened, latticed porch come the tinkling of a mandolin and a girl's low laughter. A far-off whippoorwill mourns the loneliness of things and a nearby mocking bird celebrates their loveliness.

A little, barefoot girl drives a cow home past the twin chimneys of a burned house whose ruins are overrun with honeysuckle.

A dog barks, a baby cries and the door of a cabin opens; a young woman leans against the doorway in the subdued lamplight with one arm above her head; she looks out in the darkness for a long time until she hears the mournful whistle of a passing train. All the mystery and wonder of life is in that figure.

### *On the Bench*

Every day when it is not raining, a small crowd gathers on and around the well-whittled bench in front of Lawyer Eaton's office. The bench holds only three, but there is standing room beside it. There are three regular sitters. Number one is "Admiral" Scrap Dawson, a short, fat, cock-eyed, good-humored, middle-aged man with the rolling walk of a sailor on a stormy deck; it is this walk which earned him his title; he runs the county home by remote control. Number two is Bedford Purcell, lean, grizzled, quizzical, rough-hewn and extremely ugly; he is county coroner. Number three is "Cousin Willie" MacNeill, the benevolent, pink-cheeked, gray-haired county treasurer, who is married to a nagging woman and who is liable to say to anyone he meets, "Get married, Cousin So-and-So, multiply your joys and divide your sorrows, Cousin So-and-So," though of course sometimes he gets it reversed.

The stories these three tell are not new and untried ones; they are aged in the wood and have the flavor of old liquor, old hams, old cheese and old friends.

"Who was the stealingest man you ever knew?" Mr. Purcell asked Admiral Scrap.

"Why, it was Handsome Prince," said the admiral immediately. "You remember him, a ginger-colored, quick-stepping Nigrah, used to live next to me. Of course, he stayed in jail the best part of the time, but I'd know it when he got out because the chickens would make so much fuss at night. He'd come by to see me in the morning and ask politely, 'Boss, how did you rest last night?' I'd say, 'The chickens kept me awake. They must have smelt you.'

"Once he sold me a shroud (Admiral Scrap pronounced it "swoud") he'd stolen. A Nigrah named Ed had gone Nawth and caught consumption. When he came back down here to die, he brought the finest suit of clothes you ever saw that some rich man had given him to be buried in. Of course, I didn't know that at the time, but Handsome did. Well, sir, Handsome stole that suit off that dying man. He brought it to me to trade for rations and liquor. It was the prettiest black broadcloth suit you ever saw—millionaire goods. I asked him where he got it and of course he had a plausible tale to tell. So I traded with him and put the suit on and went to church in it.

"Well, it wasn't long before I found out I had on Ed's swoud. In fact, Ed demanded it of me and I had to give it to him. But Handsome was outdone with Ed. 'I don't see how Ed could have done that to me,' he said, 'after all them chickens I and Ed done stole together.' "

"Admiral Scrap," said one of the standees, "tell us about that time the boys took you on an excursion to Ocean View and got you tight."

"That was some of Cousin Willie's doings," said Scrap. "After I'd seen all the sights at the beach, I told Cousin Willie I had to catch the train back home. Both of us were feeling pretty good by that time. He stuck my return ticket

in my hat band and put me on the roller coaster. He told
me it was the Seaboard Air Line Shoofly ready to take me
back home."

"What did you think when it got to swooping up and
down?" somebody asked.

"Well, boys," said the admiral, "I did think that the road-
bed had got a mite rough since I come up that morning."

After the laughter had died down Admiral Scrap continued, "But I got back on Cousin Willie not long after that
when a Eyetalian come through town with a dancing bear.
He come in in the middle of a hot July day, and I knew that
Cousin Willie was taking a nap in his office with his feet up
on the desk like he always does about that time of day. So
I got the Eyetalian to let the bear in Cousin Willie's office,
and when he woke up there was the bear standing over him.
I was peeping through the window. Well, sir, Cousin Willie
sailed through that window without taking his feet from the
desk as far as I could see. He knocked me down like a
cannon ball, but it was worth it."

"The meanest man I ever knew," said Coroner Purcell,
"was old man Bull Mason. He loved money more, I believe,
than even Mr. Bluejean does. His wife inherited some money
and the old man was determined to get his hands on it. She
hid it where he couldn't find it, of course. He asked her to
lend it to him, but she refused. He begged her to tell him
where it was, but she wouldn't. Then he tried to scare her
by telling her there were robbers in the neighborhood, but
she wouldn't scare. So one night he put a sheet over his head
and went to her bed and told her he was her father's spirit
and wanted his money back. But instead of giving him the
money, she picked up a shotgun and let fire at him. She
missed him and he tried to dive out of the window but his
head hit the sash and knocked him unconscious. She got out
her needle and thread and sewed him up in a sheet and gave

him a good thrashing with a buggy whip. He never got his hands on a penny of that money. His wife died without telling a soul where she hid it. He had her embalmed and put in a coffin on casters in a vault in the back yard where he could roll her out and look at her every now and then, but she hasn't said yet where that money is."

"The sorriest man I ever knew," said Scrap, "was Delancey Richardson, Jr., unless it was his father. Neither of them ever did a lick of work. The Richardsons were a fine family, but they sure had run to seed. Mr. Richardson claimed he got wore out in the Civil War, but Delancey Junior was born wore-out. The old man's wife ran a boardinghouse— she was a mighty smart woman—and her husband and her son just set around and smoked cheroots. All the help she had was a cook, and she had to change the cook every nine months on account of Delancey Junior. Finally she got her a nice-looking, hard-working colored girl named Coralie and she decided to keep her if she could. So she said to Delancey Junior one day, 'Son, I want you to promise me to stay away from Coralie because I'm not as young as I was and I can't be changing cooks every nine months like I've been having to do.' Delancey gave her his solemn oath on the Bible that he wouldn't have anything to do with Coralie. But in nine months Coralie had to leave to have a baby. Mrs. Richardson got after Delancey Junior. 'I didn't think you'd do such a thing after you promised me on the Bible, Delancey,' she said. 'But it wasn't me, Mama,' Delancey said, 'This time it was Papa.' "

### Summer in Hastings

Summer comes to Hastings with her mighty arms overflowing with gifts—peaches, apples, pears, plums, damsons, cantaloupes, watermelons, scuppernongs, green butterbeans, red tomatoes, yellow corn. It is a time for dancing and romancing, for tennis and swimming, a double-header baseball game in the country with a picnic and a free-for-all fight thrown in without extra charge; a time for school closings and drugstore gatherings of the Lily Club; a time for jumping in the creek and going after hornyheads with a burlap seine. There is a wantonness in the lukewarm air which caresses the flesh of staid citizens and invites them to shuck their shirts and even their shoes.

When summer leaves Hastings, tobacco stalks flower idly, cornfields set up their orderly encampments and vines bow down with swollen grapes. Now and then an impatient sycamore leaf flutters to the ground. The underbrush is red with sumac and dogwood embers; the goldenrod hangs its head and even squirrels move lazily. An almost invisible veil of bronze dust descends on the green maturity of trees. Persimmons glow like miniature copper moons against the blue sky. Hay is stacked in the fields, smoke rises from tobacco barns and cattle cast long shadows in the setting sun.

## At Great-Aunt Evelina's

Our Great-aunt Evelina's fiancé, Capt. Rob Arrington, was killed in the Civil War, so she never got married. Our father used to tell us about Captain Rob to encourage us to be brave, but our mother tried to throw cold water on that sort of thing because she preferred us to be safe.

"Capt. Rob Arrington was the bravest man I ever knew or knew of," our father would say after we had finished one of Aunt Lina's enormous meals. "He had grit in his craw. Did I ever tell you what he did at the Battle of Shiloh?"

We knew but we always liked to hear the gory details repeated.

"I'll tell you. The Yankees were bombarding the Confederate trenches. Bullets and cannon balls and canister were thick as hops. Suddenly our flag was shot down. The Stars and Bars, planted on the breastworks, reeled and tottered and fell in the trench at Captain Rob's feet. He snatched it up in his arms in a second, he leaped on the breastworks and brandished it in the face of the enemy and planted it once more on the rampart to wave defiance. He fell wounded in a dozen places. Now that's what I call bravery."

"It was nothing but nervousness," our mother would say.

"We took him home and nursed him," said Aunt Lina, "and we had very little food then an invalid could eat. But I did have a little red hen who laid an egg for Robert every single day. She was the most faithful chicken I ever saw. And it wasn't long before we mended Robert and had him back in the field again. He died at Gettysburg. I've often thought I'd rather"—here she looked sideways at our mother —"be the widow of a brave man than the wife of a coward."

## Autumn in Hastings

At sunup spider webs gleam on hedgerows, morning glories glow on bean poles, and old hounds seek the sunny side of the house. At noon daisies and goldenrod light the roadsides, scalybarks plop on the ground, and acorns crunch underfoot. At night the cricket sings on the hearth, blue supper smoke rises from chimneys, and the harvest moon gilds the spent fields. It is the time of pumpkins, apples, scuppernongs, zinnias, dahlias, chrysanthemums. Cotton whitewashes the fields, pine cones roost like little turkeys, brambles rustle in the breeze, and the red fox streaks across brown hills ahead of spotted hounds. There is a smell of burning brush in the air, and loads of tobacco rumble to market under faded bed quilts.

On the hills the crucibles of color have boiled over. Under

the blue sky there are green pines, furs and cedars; golden poplars, elms and Judas trees; red dogwoods, oaks and blackgums; maples imitate parrots with red, green and yellow plumage.

## On the Porch

The beautiful young woman often wondered what her very old Cousin Eugenia thought about as she sat on her porch alone every warm evening at twilight and gazed across the darkening little valley on the edge of town. The old lady had been a great beauty in her day—which was before the Civil War—and even now her face had the charm of serenity.

As the young woman, Lucy, approached the big, square, old, three-story, red brick house surrounded by huge boxwoods, it was just light enough for her to see her cousin in her usual place.

Lucy opened the wrought-iron gate and entered the yard. She had been in the old house countless times before and had been enchanted from childhood by the marvelous things in it—the spiral staircase in the hall, with its Chinese Chippendale woodwork; the portraits staring at her wherever she went; the parlor overflowing with things which Cousin Eugenia had collected here and there in the world, including the Brussels carpet where the roses were wearing thin at last, the little painting of the Madonna which was a present from the Orsini family, the grandfather clock which used to show the phases of the moon and chime the hours and quarter-hours, the framed letters from John Paul Jones and John Howard Paine, the little heart and cross which were whittled out of pine by General Sam Houston and given by him to Cousin Eugenia when she was a young girl, the jeweled cane which Santa Anna left behind him hurriedly in the war for Texan independence, the two heavy silver casters which decorated the long, mahogany table and which opened ingeniously when one turned a knob to disclose a circle of mysterious bottles and an inscription saying, "Patent Applied For, 1850."

"Cousin Eugenia," Lucy said, "would you mind if I asked you what you think about here on the porch?"

"Why, no, Sugarpie. I think about what all old people think about—the good old days, and the bad old days."

"I've always heard you had a hundred proposals," Lucy said, as if it were a leading question. She could believe it was true after looking at the portrait of Cousin Eugenia as a girl at Montmorenci, with her ermine fur and her mother-of-pearl opera glasses which always seemed too ostentatious for the sweet, calm face.

"Oh, proposals were a dime a dozen in those days, Sugarpie. I was not as pretty as you are, but I did have ninety-seven."

"And I've had only three," wailed Lucy.

"Ah, but you've got the man you love, Lucy, and he will take you with him wherever his paper sends him and you will see the world and the world will love you."

"Your world," said Lucy, remembering that Cousin Eugenia's husband had been Ambassador to the Court of Rome and Naples.

"It was never exactly my world, Sweetness, I took after my mother. She was born in a log cabin and brought up in a mansion with lots of servants to wait on her, in a society that spent the time drinking, gambling and playing politics, but she was really a Puritan; I think she had to be because she was left a widow at twenty-one, and she had the burden of the plantation on her shoulders. She always said that kind of life couldn't last, and it didn't.

"She had her troubles. The business burdens she could share with her overseers, but the human burdens she couldn't

share with anyone except the Lord. She took it on herself to
doctor her colored people, act as judge between them, patch
up their quarrels, nurse them at all hours when they were
sick, teach them the Bible, and there was no end to it. She
often told me there was a lot of truth in Mrs. Stowe's book."

"You don't call them slaves?" Lucy asked.

"No, it is a bad word, Honey. Her people were on her
conscience. There they were multiplying all the time, and
her troubles multiplying with them. What worried her most
were not those on her plantation in North Carolina where
she could keep an eye on them, but those on her plantation
in Georgia where she couldn't see them more than once a
year or so and couldn't tell what was happening to their
bodies or their souls. She couldn't watch over them, she
wouldn't sell them of course, and she couldn't free them any
more than you could turn children out to graze. And every
year there would be a new batch of them to worry about.
She said many a time that it would all come to a bad end,
and I think she was relieved when it did.

"When I met Mr. Mason at a ball in Washington—he was
on a visit home from Italy, and a very handsome man he was
with his black beard and black eyes—I fell in love with him
at first sight. When he paid his addresses, my mother didn't
approve of him, she thought him too wild—he had been married once before, you know—so she told him he would do
better to sue for an ambassadorship to the kingdom of
heaven. He told her that was exactly what he was doing in
asking for my hand, but she was not amused.

"However, we had a grand wedding in the ballroom at
Montmorenci and went to live in Rome. That was just before the war. My mother bought this house in town and
rented her plantations to Colonel Greene, a gentleman she
knew she could trust to look after her people with kindness
and firmness."

"Perhaps she couldn't bear to live in Montmorenci," said Lucy, "after you left."

"She was very fond of me," said Cousin Eugenia, "though she was not one to show her feelings. It is all in her journal —her love, her lonesomeness, her perplexity and her prayers. I thought of her so often in Rome—especially at twilight, while I looked at that beautiful skyline, with its domes and towers and obelisks, from the Piazza del Popolo or the Pincian Hill—and of how good and strong and kind she was.

"When the war broke out, Mr. Mason came home because he thought his place was here. His heart was with the South because he was a Southerner, but his mind was with the Union because he thought secession was foolish.

"So we moved back to his home in Tennessee, and when the Union Army captured the town, he told me he was going to put the Union flag up over our house and give the officers a dinner; many of them were old friends of his. I begged him not to, but he did. Then he joined the Union Army as a major and not long after that he was killed. I took my son, who was two years old, and made my way back through the Yankee lines to my mother's house. During the war my mother died. Everything was lost by then, except what we have here. It was a hard time for me. I took my dead sister's children in the house with me. They thought I was stingy. There was not always enough to eat, so I would say at the table:

> Of a little, take a little,
>   Mind what you do,
> Of a little, have a little,
>   So the rest can have some too.

"I kept the post office here for a while during President Johnson's administration, and I had a pension as the widow of a Union officer. But the other women looked at me as if I had murdered their sons or husbands. It was hard on my

son, too, when he became old enough to find out that his
father had fought on the other side. Of course, it was a cruel
time, but I hold it against grown people who take out their
hatred on a child. So I gave up the pension and the post
office and started teaching school. At first the neighbors
would not trust their children with me, but gradually they
did, and I tried to teach them to read and think, to know
what is right and what is trifling or trashy. And all the while
it was a great trouble to me to think of the waste of boys and
girls—so few could keep up their education and so many
would throw themselves away in ignorance and narrowness,
laziness and boredom and drunkenness. But things are better
now, Sugarpie. The bright ones like you are going to college
and getting out to see the world.

"So that's what I think about sitting here on the porch
after sunset."

### Winter in Hastings

The picture is monotonously outlined in browns, grays
and blacks, relieved here and there with green of pines and
cedars. A slate-gray sky presses on dun fields in which coffee-
colored stalks of last year's cotton and tobacco stand around
shabbily. Yet there is the noble architecture of oaks.

When snows come they are like guests so unsure of their
welcome that they prepare to leave as soon as they arrive.
Often they fail to cover the broomstraw, though they tuft it
with fraudulent white blossoms: they put nightcaps on fence
posts and paint streaks of white on the windy side of telephone poles. Their thin veil hardly hides the phosphorescent
green of coming cover crops. But roofs are uniformly white,
the countryside is shrouded, and chimney smoke spreads out
indolently between heaven and earth like a gray thought in
a gray shade.

# 4

## Uncle Remus Spake Queen's English

Southern dialect is neither Southern nor dialect. What is generally regarded as "nigger talk" or hillbilly lingo is far more likely to be the Queen's English of the time of Shakespeare and Marlowe, Addison and Swift, Pope and Dryden, or Dr. Johnson and Boswell.

If Sir Walter Raleigh, Uncle Remus, Queen Elizabeth I and an old-timey black mammy should ever in any seance attend a faculty tea of an average American university, Uncle Remus, Elizabeth, Sir Walter and Mammy would understand one another well enough, but they would have no idea what the faculty members were talking about.

"Ez de tale was gun to me, I gin it unter you," said Uncle Remus to the little boy. Sir Walter would have understood this because it would probably have been pretty close to what he would have said himself. So would Robert Burns—"our billies gi'en us a' a jink."

If Mammy should say to Elizabeth—to set her at her ease—"Honey, hit don't make no never mind," her majesty would feel very much at home, because, in the first place, Elizabeth

57

habitually used *hit* for *it*. Professor George P. Wilson, former secretary of the American Dialect Society, states in a
chapter on folk speech in the *Frank C. Brown Collection of
North Carolina Folk Lore,* that he noted "in thirty-two of
her letters fifty-nine uses of *hit* and twenty-two of *it, e.g.,*
'and make hit plaine that we delt plainly.'" In the second
place, double negatives were the Virgin Queen's delight; if
there was one thing she loved better than a double negative
it was a triple, or even a quadruple, one—doubtless they came
in handy for courtiers who, like Sir Walter, wouldn't take no
for an answer.

Suppose a Southern swain should croon to his lady love
beneath the magnolia tree in the moonlight, "Linda Lou,
Ah love you and Ah want you to be mah wife. Let us jine
hands and heahts." Would he be talking Southern? Yes, but
he would also be using the speech (though certainly not the
prosody) of the immaculate Pope and the fastidious Dryden.
Let us not forget that when Alexander Pope wrote in his
*Essay on Criticism:*

> Good nature and good sense must ever join;
> To err is human, to forgive divine,

he had no doubt that his verses rhymed. Of course, they did.
And, of course, the use of *Ah* for I and *mah* for my comes
not from darkest Africa but from fashionable London a century or so ago. So do the dropped *r*'s and *g*'s of Southern
speech.

Thus, as Mr. Wilson points out, the following words,
which are looked on in modern society with holy horror,
possess the authority of antiquity and the imprimatur of the
masters of English, at least from Ben Jonson to Samuel Johnson:

*Afeared* for afraid (Pepys, *Diary,* 1668: "I became *afeared* to
stay there long")

*Arter* for after (this makes the nursery rhyme of Jack and Jill
come out as it should)

*Ast* for asked

*Back* for address, as to back a letter

*Cowcumber* for cucumber

*Blowed* for blown (Shakespeare, *Henry V:* "I would have
*blowed* up the town")

*Catched* for caught (Milton, *Paradise Lost:* ". . . and dire form
*catched* by contagion")

*Fitten* for fitting

*His'n* and *her'n* for his and hers (as in the old rhyme) :

> "He that prigs what isn't *his'n*
> When he's cotched is sent to prison;
> She that prigs what isn't *her'n*
> At the treadmill take a turn";

*Ingern* for onion

*Git* for get

*Dahlin* for darling

*Yallah* for yellow

*Chainy* for china

*Obleege* for oblige

*Learn* for teach (Coverdale's Psalms, 1535: "Lead me in thy
truth and *lerne* me")

*Mought* for might (Bacon: "Such a vast sea mought cause it")

*Jine* for join, *bile* for boil, *pizen* for poison and so on

*Mush-million* for muskmelon (of all things!)

It would be a good bet that when Dizzy Dean says a base-
runner "slud" into second base he is using a past tense of the
verb *slide* which was once fashionable in London. Lord
Berners' translation of Froissart (1523) puts it this way: "He
slode and fell downe."

But why labor the point? Southern talk has aristocratic
ancestry and can trace it on the dialectal family tree.

How then did it come about that the real stuff is now
looked on as the spurious, if not for the human propensity

to "give to dross that is a little gilt more praise than gold o'erdusted"?

The rule is that the colonists stick closer to their mother tongue than the homefolks do. London may adopt new-fangled ways of talking, but Possum Holler abides by the old way; it removes not the linguistic landmarks which the fathers have set. So when a hillbilly at a baseball game tells you the score is "nary-nary in the seventh with we-uns to bat," he may be speaking a purer (or at least more venerable) brand of English than you give him credit for.

"The South is divided and uneven in speech," writes Hans Kurath in *Modern Philology,* "Tidewater Virginia is southern English in speech, the Piedmont and the mountain country of the Atlantic states strongly Scotch; Georgia and the old Southwest mixed the two in stock and speech—the latter type predominating in the upper South, the former in the lower South."

Some writers go further and trace kinship not only in a taste for words but also in a taste for literature. Thus William Aspenwall Bradley in *Harper's Magazine* (1915) asserts that "when the mountaineer begins to read at all, he displays so marked a preference for Shakespeare that it is invariably the works of that poet that have most frequently to be rebound in any library to which he has access. The reason he himself gives for this predilection is that the things Shakespeare makes his characters do seem so 'natural.'"

It may be doubted that the average literate mountaineer is such a rabid Shakespeare fan, but it is plausible enough that Shakespeare's characters act "natural" to him, considering what a violent lot the sweet bard of Avon's characters were, from Hamlet and Hotspur to Goneril and Lady Macbeth. Certainly the Martins and the Coys ("who took up family feudin when they'd meet") would see nothing unusual in the goings-on of the Montagues and the Capulets.

But why did the South hold to the old forms of speech so much more tenaciously than the the North did? Public education and Noah Webster must bear a heavy responsibility for that. Late in the eighteenth century Webster published his famous spelling books, in which he urgd the Yankees not to say (as they had been saying) *thar* for there, *gal* for girl, *comin* for coming, *apun* for apron, *bust* for burst, *ax* for ask, *kiver* for cover, *shet* for shut, *sperit* for spirit, and so on.

The South, of course, paid no attention to the upstart Webster, but the other parts of the country took him seriously as the Emily Post of the Word.

This was the same Noah Webster who sanctioned the use of *you was* for you were and *them* horses for those horses (under the delusion that *them* was equivalent to the German *dem*.) He insisted to his dying day that Southerners simply did not understand grammar, and wrote in his diary: "O, New England, how superior are thy inhabitants in morals, literature, civility, and industry!"

### One Way to Tell

One way to tell whether a person is a Southerner—so they say—is to ask him to speak this sentence: "Mrs. Alexander Cooper's daughter Mary was at school Tuesday."

If he says, "Miz Ellexandah Coopuh's (oo as in book) daughter Mayry was at school Tewsday," he is from "de lan' ob cotton."

But if he says, "Misses Alexanderr Coo-per's daughter Merry was at school Toosday," he is a Yankee or something, and his speech "bewrayeth" him.

Yet perhaps there is a Southern dialect, and if so, here is a sample of it from Bill Sharpe in his *State* (Raleigh, N.C.) *Magazine:*

For several weeks I felt sort o' shacklin, but recently I've been right peart, so I reckon I ain't got no right to do any grossin.

Maybe I've been workin too hard, reddin up the house and gittin sass out of the garden. That kind of work almost always gives me the all-overs.

John don't help me much, because he's right busy barnin, so I don't fault him none. And then, to add to my troubles, the baby swallowed a latch pin. He's the one that imitates his father so much. Last week he ate a scimption of leather britches and they made him sick. I get in such a swivet sometimes that I really don't know what I'm doin.

Our house is fernent the woods, near the branch. It has a nice gallery which is a mite antigodlin. John bought a horse last week that turned out to be a cribber. I blessed him out about it, but he just laughed and bussed me. He never pays me no mind. Maybe one of these days I'll get my go-poke and visit my sister Minnie for a few weeks. She's sort o' mincy and she has a passle of young uns, but I think I'd enjoy the change. She lives on the other side of the pocosin.

It would be tempting, but unfair, to call dialect "fossilized" language. It is too full of life for that—the virility, beauty, humor, pathos, color and vulgarity of life are all there, and all are intensified. Dialect has, in Baconian phrase, "some sparkles of liberty, spirit and edge" to it. It says things right.

There is nothing mechanical or contrived about true dialect. The counterfeits, which are built like a box, are easily shown up by the genuine article, which grows like a tree.

Such "Americanisms" as *cavu* (ceiling and visibility unlimited), *ebaw* (even birds are walking), *snafu* (situation normal, all fouled up), *trike* (tricycle), *beefcake* on the *telecast* (a display of masculine pulchritude on the television receiver), *butterlegger* and *helimail* are obviously contrived, and as lifeless as tin.

Genuine dialect sometimes has a beauty all its own. For

proof note these samples of North Carolina talk lovingly collected by Mr. Wilson:

"So fur back in them coves you had to keep wipin' at the shadows"; "Jane has pensy eyes"; "as pure as the jest of God"; "morn gloam" (the first light of morning); "peep-by-night" (a flower that opens only at night); "evening glom" (the melancholy close of day); "rain seed" (mottled clouds indicative of rain); "sun-ball" (the sun); "quietus" (the calm that comes to one after death, used in pity by an old woman about a wild animal that had been killed by dogs); "element" (the sky).

This is patently finer stuff than correct English.

Dialect is indeed a living thing, coming from the lips of the people, like the soul, which in Dante's vision comes forth from the hand of God, laughing, weeping and frolicking like a little child.

The folks who live on North Carolina's Outer Banks use a dialect which probably goes all the way back to Elizabethan Devonshire and may well be the same one which caused the other courtiers to rib Sir Walter at the great queen's court, for he, according to a contemporary, "spake broad Devonshire to his dying day."

The most noticeable thing about the speech of the Outer Banker is his use of *oi* for *i*. So instead of saying "high tide in Hyde County," he will say (or used to until he became corrupted by too much book larnin), "hoigh toide in Hoyde County." Try to put one off a bus and he'll say, "Oi paid moy money to roide and Oi'm going to roide." He comes by his speech legitimately, for an ancient map of Roanoke Island spells it "Oisland."

One day at Nags Head I was on the ocean side of the bank and wanted to get over to the sound side, but I didn't remember where the road was and I didn't want to get stuck in the sand, so I asked an old fellow leaning against a filling station tank, "How do you git over to the sound soide?"

He knew I had no license to use his language. "Boy Gawd," he said, "you jest roide over there."

The wonderful thing about dialect is that it can often supply you with a more fitting word for what you want to say than the dictionary or thesaurus can.

For a long time I had the good fortune to have in my home a cook, maid, nurse, family retainer and dear friend who was an old-timey Negro with the lovely name of Violet Christmas (naturally she had a cousin named Early Christmas) who was illiterate but who had so much "mother wit" and possessed such a genius for making up words that I often had the feeling that I was privileged to be present at the birth of dialect.

For instance, my wife, who comes from Canada and who in a way inherited Violet by marriage, asked Violet why she had not learned to read and write. Violet explained to her that she had quit school as a child because her teacher warned her that if she kept on it might "give her a tumult on the brain."

One day Violet was going down the street and met a proud couple wheeling their first-born in a baby carriage. "Violet," the father asked, "who do you think the baby looks more like, me or its mother?" Violet, always diplomatic, answered, "I think it's a blemish of both."

Violet always referred to typhoid fever as "terrified" fever, the Oxford Group as the "Oxford Droop," kidnap as "catnip," a magnolia tree as a "linoleum" tree, and the chimes of the grandfather clock as the "charms." "Charms" so used must mean a comminglement of sweet sounds. See Milton: "But neither breath of morn when she ascends with charm of earliest birds . . ." from that grand speech of Eve to Adam in *Paradise Lost,* beginning "with thee conversing I forget all time" (as if she had anybody else to converse with)!

What a simple primrose by the river's brim was to Violet is unknown, but a poached egg was sometimes a "proached" and sometimes a "post-toasted" egg.

On one occasion my wife asked her to call up the grocer and order some "Vienna sausages, Wesson oil and spaghetti." Violet, of course, told the grocer to send Miss Marion some "piano sausages, wizard oil and fergit it." The grocer, of course, knew what she meant, and the order came through perfectly.

A lot of dialect spills over into humor. Thus a *straddlebug* is a politician. *Mugwump* carries its obvious connotation. A *snollygoster* is a fellow who "wants office regardless of party, platform or principles and who, whenever he wins, gets there by sheer force of monumental talknophical assumnacy." A snollygoster would be likely to say in the course of an address, "I wishes to expatiate and I wants what I say to be recorded in the archives of gravity."

A *claphat* woman is a hasty one.

A *slipper-slide* is a shoe horn.

*Whistle-britches* is a small boy proud of his first pair of trousers.

A woman at the *whitleather stage* is likely to be a tough customer.

*Briar-patch chillun* are not quite legitimate. Other names for them are *ditch-edge* or *long o' de paat* (path) *chillun;* they were *born on the wrong side of the blanket* and are *wood's colts* or *outsiders.*

*Giggle soup* is liquor.

*Journey-proud* applies to one who can't stop talking about where he has been.

A *shotgun* house is built all in one row.

A *smidgen* is a little and a *slue* is a lot.

*Whiffledust* is what you sprinkle on the threshold of the court-room so that your lawyer will *put you on the ground* again.

A *writermarouster* is a court order of ejectment.

*Burnt-Tail Jinny* is the wife of Will o' the Wisp or Jack o' Lantern.

Dialect has beauty in it as well as humor. *Blackberry winter* or *dogwood winter* is a cold snap in early spring.

A *lavish* of fruit is a *God's plenty*.

*Ice pebbles* are hail.

*Misty-moist* weather threatens rain.

*Dusty-dark* is the time just before the twilight sky turns from gray to blue.

From *kin-see* to *cain't-see* is a full day.

The heat waves on the road are *witch water*.

The *devil's riding horse* is the praying mantis.

A *guy-scooter-sky* is a steer with hind legs longer than fore legs for mountain grazing.

A *snake doctor* is a dragonfly.

And *shoe bread* is a thin sandwich of bread and bacon which you slip into your shoe to entice a valuable dog away from home.

But dialect is more at home in a story than a treatise, and the true business of this living language is not to "rust un-burnished" but to "shine in use."

So let us see how much dialect we can put to work in a story. It is a story told by Old Man Jenkins to a young fellow and it is called

### A DARK HOUSE AND A BLOODY FIGHT

Your Uncle Buck was as bowdacious a man as ever I see. When they made him they broke the mold.

One spring day about dusty-dark he come a-bilin up to my shack and hollered, "Come on, Jinks, we gotto go to a infare over to the Fescues. Evergreen's a-goin to be thar."

I went out in the yard and thar was Buck in the sulky with

his roan stallion Grover Cleveland hitched up to it and a jug of the o-be-joyful on the seat by him. He was dressed in his Sunday-go-to-meetin clothes. "The sap's risin, Jinks!" he yelled.

He looked to me like he was in a franzy. "You better stay way from Evergreen, Buck," I said. "You know good and well she jest got married to Jason Turnipseed and I ain't a-goin to have no doins with that. You're goin to git yourself in bad trouble and I don't want no part on it."

"Don't you gimme no backjaw, Jinks. I know Evergreen's been married for a fortnight to a eight-dollar-a-month counter-hopper and breast-pin thief. He ain't fitten for her. She needs a he-man like me, and I'm goin to take her away from him tonight if it's the last thing I do on earth."

So we clum in the sulky and Grover lit a rag for the shindig at the Fescues. Old Lady Fescue—that's Evergreen's mama—always said, "Every gal ought to have two babies before she gits married, it settles 'em down so," and her fambly pretty well practiced what she preached. Her folks changed their names from time to time accordin to what they had of this world's goods. When they didn't have nothin at all, they called themselves Pendergrasses; when they accumulated some personal property like chickens and chairs, they got to be Searuggs; and when they got titlement to a piece of land, they come to be Fescues.

When we got to the Fescues—it was a long, low, shotgun house on Ripshin Ridge above Lickskillet Creek—we dreened the jug of white mule, tied Grover so fur out in the woods nobody would see him, and went in at the front door.

It was the biggest fooraw anybody ever hearn tell of. The front room was playing tendergarden that night for the folks that had brung their younguns along. They was chaps in dresses and in hippins, teenintsey babies, breast babies, arm babies, lap babies, knee babies, porch babies and yard babies,

not to mention briar-patch chillun, all bawlin' their heads
off. Thar was a pair of twins thar that didn't have a freckle's
difference between 'em.

Miss Martha Harris, an old maid at the whiteleather stage,
was mindin 'em and she shore had a passel of younguns
trinklin around underfoot. Some of the slappin-high ones
had a bad case of the smarts, so she told 'em the booger man
would get at 'em with his larrows to ketch meddlers if they
weren't more mannerable, but they jest kept on carryin on.
The place looked like a hooraw's nest.

But the back room was where the fun was. You could hear
the fiddlin and stompin and squealin and hollerin a country
mile.

There was a slue of people thar, a regular go-and-come, but
Buck didn't have eyes for nobody but Evergreen. He looked
all over for her but he couldn't locate her nowhere. How-
somever, he did find old Mrs. Fescue settin by the liquor kag
with the top knocked in and the dipper hangin out. So he
went over to her and says, "Where's Evergreen, Miz Fescue?"

"Well, if it ain't Mr. McIllhenny," says the old bag.
"Here's lookin to you and towards you; if I hadn't a seed
you I wouldn't a knowed you. What's the good word, Buck?
I hain't seed you in a coon's age. What you been doin with
yerself?"

"Oh, jest a-chawin of tobaccer, a-smokin of cheroots, a
eatin of sardines and a romancin around. You musta put
the big pot in the little one for this shindig, Miz Fescue."

"Are you feelin good tonight, Mr. McIllhenny?"

"I'm a-feelin like a turkey in young corn, here today and
soon gone, Miz Fescue. The sap's risin in me. I'm mean as
all outdoors tonight. I'm goin to raise hell and put a chunk
under it. I'm walkin in high cotton. Burnt-tail Jinny led
me here. Hell and high water couldn't stop me. A gully-
washer, nubbin-stretcher and toad-floater couldn't keep me

away tonight. I'm a gallivantin galoot with the goies. I'm sweetheartin tonight. Where's Evergreen?"

"Buck," said Mrs. Fescue solemnly, "ain't you as drunk as a skunk at a moonshine still?"

"I swear before God, Miz Fescue, I ain't drinked enough to put in a baby's eye. I'm jest sweatin. I'm hot as a nigger in hell writin a love letter and tryin to spell. Where's Evergreen? I'll be a nervous wretch if I don't find her."

"She just went out to take Jason back home. He wasn't feelin so peart, and I don't think he was enjoyin hisself."

"That tune-heistin, psalm-singin, bible-backed son of a bitch," said Buck, "ain't got no call to be married to Evergreen."

"Well, now he is sorta puny," said Mrs. Fescue, "but whyn't you bruise around the womenfolks and git you another gal?"

"Where's Evergreen?" said Buck.

"Well, Buck, if you must know," said Mrs. Fescue, "she's comin back to the ruckus as soon as she gits Jason to bed."

"She's my eyeballs," said Buck. "When she comes in a room I feel fantified and feather-legged." He put the dipper in the kag and took him a man's-sized drink.

Pretty soon Evergreen come back. But she warn't by herself. She was with Bull-o'-the-Woods Heptinstall.

Evergreen was a teen-aged, brown-haired, blue-eyed, well-rounded gal with a come-hither look if I ever seen one. Bull was a black-haired, strappin young fellow, about six foot three and right much of a man; he'd make two of Buck.

Buck stood there, tore between love and hate. "Jest look at her!" he said half to hisself. "She'll melt like caramel in a man's mouth. She's radiatin love like a king heater. She's exudin honey like a overflowin bee-tree. She's got a heart like lightwood and I'm her match."

Then he took a look at Bull Heptinstall, and it pretty near

give him a double duck fit. "Look at him," said Buck.
"Jason knows good and well Bull's bad after women. He
ain't got no business lettin a man of Bull's character go out
in the nighttime with Evergreen. It's—it's *immoral,* God
damn it, that's what it is! I'll knock him looser quickern he
kin say God with his mouth open."

With that he navigated kinda slaunchways over to where
Bull and Evergreen were.

"Bull," he said, comin straight to the pint, "you know
what I'm a-goin to do to you?"

"Well no, I don't," said Bull, "but if you feel froggish,
hop."

"You're a gone goslin, Bull, I'm a winchester and a stem-
winder. I'm a catawampus from the whangdoodle's nest;
and you're so low you could walk under a trundle bed with a
silk hat on."

"Don't you be castin no epitaphs at me," said Bull. "I'm
a mean man myself. I got Western blood in me. I'm full of
the old spizzerinctum. I'll saw your water off if you mess
with me. I'll cut your body up in small pieces and send 'em
to the coroner in a crocus sack, collect. I'm borin with a
big auger. I'm a ring-tail tooter, iron backbone, steel ribs,
suckled by a wolf with four rows of tits and holes punched
for more."

*"Gentlemun! Gentlemun!"* Mrs. Fescue shrieked.

Evergreen stood there with her breath comin fast and her
eyes shinin. "I ain't had so much fun," she said, "since the
hogs et Grandma."

"I'll make you call for the calf rope, Bull," said Buck.
"I'll cold-cock you. I'll *alter* you."

"And if you say another crooked word to me," Bull
shouted, "I'll lay you flatter'n the panel of my hand."

"Ram's horn, damn you!" hollered Buck, and the fight
was on.

Bull fotch Buck a lick side his haid that made his comple-
ments change. Folks gathered round thick as hops. Buck
hauled off to give Bull a haymaker and just at that time a
humpbacked fellow named Littlebit blew out the lamp and
hollered, "A dark house and a bloody fight!"

And that's the way it was, my boy, when your Uncle Buck
was gallivantin around, back in the good old days—more
liquor, more fightin, more women! Sometimes, you know, I
think it was almost *immoral!*

# PART II

---

*WHAT IS THE SOUTH DOING?*

# 5

## "Save Your Confed'rit Money, Boys, the South Will Rise Again"

The agricultural South is beating its plowshares into spindles, and its pruning hooks into isotopes. Factory chimneys are replacing cornstalks. Yesterday's cotton plantation is today's synthetics manufacturing plant.

An inquisitive New York lawyer, vacationing at Nags Head on North Carolina's Outer Banks, once saw a native fishing from a rotting pier and asked him a queer question: "How much money, my friend, do you make a month?" The fisherman, who lived from day to day like the lilies of the field or the birds of the air, had never considered such a problem; he had not the faintest notion how much he made a month, or even a year, but he wasn't going to admit it to a stranger, so he said, "These fish don't bite by the month."

His was the voice of the vanishing South. The difference between the agricultural South and the industrial South is that the former never knew how much it made, while the latter knows very well because it gets paid every week.

Furthermore, the industrial South has steady customers who "bite by the month." When an American citizen from

75

Maine to California smokes a cigarette, steps on the gas, wipes his hand with a towel, puts on a shirt, or a sock, or takes a drink—soft or hard—the chances are that he is using a product from the South. When a woman puts on her clothes in the morning or pulls up a blanket at night, it is not unlikely that she has bought something "made in the South."

Some sixty years ago Henry W. Grady of Georgia complained that the Southern agrarian economy had to import practically every manufactured product it used. In a speech at Boston he described the funeral of a "one-gallus" Georgia cracker:

"They cut through solid marble to make his grave, and yet a little tombstone they put above him was from Vermont. They buried him in the heart of a pine forest, and yet the pine coffin was imported from Cincinnati. They buried him within touch of an iron mine, and yet the nails in his coffin and the iron in the shovel that dug his grave were imported from Pittsburgh. They buried him by the side of the best sheep-grazing country on the earth, and yet the wool in the coffin bands and the coffin bands themselves were brought from the North. They buried him in a New York coat and a Boston pair of shoes and a pair of breeches from Chicago and a shirt from Cincinnati. The South didn't furnish a thing on earth for that funeral but the corpse and the hole in the ground."

Today, as the Southern Association of Science and Industry points out, the Georgia farmer's relatives could have buried him in style with the aid of over two thousand Dixie manufacturers and "without a single Yankee embellishment." They could select a tombstone from thirteen manufacturers in seven Southern states; a fancy casket with nylon lining from twenty-one Southern manufacturers; nails, shovels and other hardware from one hundred and forty-nine Southern steel fabricators, or one hundred and one big foundries; the materials for the coffin bands from more than one thousand Southern textile plants; they could dress him in clothes made in one or more of six hundred and sixty-two apparel plants from Florida to Kentucky, and in shoes made in any of the seventy-two shoe manufacturing plants from Arkansas to Maryland, shined with polish from Tennessee. The hearse could come from Alabama, rolling on tires and tubes from Louisiana or Mississippi, and be propelled by gasoline from Texas. Today the South would furnish everything including the hole in the ground.

This does not mean that the South has anything like the amount or diversity of industry that some other regions have. It does mean that the South is expanding its old industry, attracting new industry and narrowing the gap which has separated its standard of living from the standards of wealthier sections.

How the gap is being narrowed is indicated by the fact that, since two million Southerners have been placed on new and steady payrolls, Southern income has been skyrocketing. So has the income of the rest of the country. But per capita income and various other economic indices have been rising faster in the South than in the nation in general. In the *1952 Annual Report* of the Southern Company, based on sixteen Southern states and the District of Columbia, note the comparative rates of increase between 1940 and 1951:

| Indices | South | U.S. |
|---|---|---|
| Per capita increase | 218% | 175% |
| Bank deposits | 237% | 145% |
| Life insurance in force | 157% | 109% |
| Value of manufactured products | 376% | 330% |
| Value added by manufacturing | 352% | 312% |
| Electric energy sales | 217% | 168% |

### *One Multi-Million Dollar Industry A Day*

During the years 1951 and 1952, the South added on each working day an average of one multi-million dollar industry to its economy.

The 1952 Directory of the Southern Association of Science and Industry lists more than 12,500 manufacturing plants in the South which employ 50 or more workers, including "1,001 textile mills, 662 apparel plants, 620 food canning and processing plants, 617 lumber and woodworking plants, 377 hosiery mills, 301 wood furniture plants, 231 dairy products plants, 299 bakeries, 191 printing and publishing plants, 161 meat packing plants and 149 steel fabricators."

The growth of the chemical industry in the South is indicated by the fact that in 1952 there were 131 manufacturers of industrial chemicals and 151 major petroleum refineries in the region. In recent years the chemical industry has been locating more than half its new plants in the South; Du Pont has placed almost all of its plants there since the Second World War; indeed, chemicals have apparently taken the lead as the South's biggest and most profitable industrial activity.

In the past twenty years the South has been transformed from "the nation's number one economic problem" to the nation's greatest economic opportunity. It has moved its stand from "the wailing wall to the industrial research laboratory." *Time* magazine calls it "history's first enlightened industrial revolution."

North Carolina, with its tremendous textile, tobacco and furniture industries, has been leading this revolution, but other Southern states are hard on its heels, and Texas may have overtaken Tarheelia by the time this is in print.

Some impression of the scope and diversity of the South's

industrialization may be gained by the following facts gathered at random:

McIntosh, Alabama (pop. 100) woke up to find an $8,000,000 soda and chlorine plant, together with a $40,000,000 steam plant, in its municipal lap. Gabe, Kentucky (pop. 40) was startled to find itself the home of a $35,000,000 ethylene glycol (whatever that may be) manufactory.

Within a thirty-mile radius of Clemson, South Carolina (pop. 435), there sprang up a $6,000,000 J. P. Stevens cotton mill, a $6,500,000 Gerrish Milliken rayon-nylon plant, a $4,000,000 Deering Milliken worsted and nylon finishing plant and a $12,000,000 Owens-Corning fiber glass mill. But that was a year or so ago, and doubtless others have sprung up since.

In Pisgah Forest near Asheville, North Carolina, the Ecusta plant is making the paper in which billions of cigarettes will be rolled and the cellophane to cover the packages. And at Rolla, North Carolina, on Turtle Mountain, Chippewa Indians are working at a new ordnance plant turning out a product vital to national defense but so small that the annual output would hardly fill a suitcase; it consists of jewel bearings essential to precision instruments in bombers, battleships and artillery shells.

All over the South, but especially in Virginia and the Carolinas, the woods are full of mills making synthetic fabrics with strange names like dynel, orlon, saran, Reevon, acrilan, duplan and dacron. The South has discovered that it does not have to imitate a worm and start off with a cocoon to make a stocking or a slip.

The Old South of slave labor and the later South of near-slave labor is now the new South which is substituting "brains for brawn." In the Southern petro-chemical industry the investment exceeds $30,000 per worker. Some of the newest plants are virtually automatic in operation. A syn-

thetic fiber plant in Alabama, according to H. McKinley
Conway, Jr., director of the Southern Association of Science
and Industry, "will employ only a few hundred workers to
turn out millions of pounds of fibers annually, and will employ more people in its research laboratories and administra-
tive offices than in the manufacturing plant."

In Hartsville, South Carolina an industry, operated by the
Coker family and called the Southern Novelty Company or
Sonoco, manufactures its own machinery and make with it
all sorts of pasteboard gadgets, such as spools, cones and bob-
bins, for the textile business all over the world. It also makes
containers for various industries. Its latest product is a large
tube which is used as a form for molding concrete pillars for
buildings, piers, et cetera. Its trucks carry its products north
and bring back old newspapers in bales to make more gadgets.
So a headline about Willie "The Actor" Sutton or Georgi
Malenkov may be part of a newspaper today and the forma-
tive influence of a concrete pier tomorrow.

Sparked by TVA's low-cost power, Tennessee is garnering
a good deal of new industry. The big Kingsport Press and the
Eastman Kodak plant are samples of what might be called
settled industry in Tennessee, but the state is encouraging a
lot of experiments in manufacturing, such as soap from waste
tobacco, textiles from milk, rubber from soy beans and alco-
hol from wood waste.

While much of the new industry in the South has gone
hayseed and taken to the sticks, not all of it has. The newer
Southern cities are welcoming the industrial order with outstretched arms, as a matter of course. Atlanta, Georgia, overflowing with neon lights and traffic, seems to be trying to
outshine and outswarm New York City; it not only makes a
number of things from mechanical pencils to bombers, but
acts as a distribution center for the South. Birmingham, Ala-

bama, the steel city of the South over which a gigantic statue of Vulcan presides, got tired of being too dependent on steel and iron, wherefore its Committee of One Hundred was organized to help it get diversified industries to manufacture everything from steel ingots to watch springs. Houston, Texas has moved so fast in commerce and industry as to be fabulous; "the city of five hundred rich and poor millionaires" is now the nation's second biggest seaport, though it is fifty miles from the seacoast. In Houston, as James Street says, "it takes a yacht, two or three airplanes, a few ranches, plus about $20,000,000 in cash to move in the stratosphere of the really rich."

Perhaps this sort of thing is what is to be expected of the brash cities of the New South which are hardly dry behind the ears. But it comes as a shock to see the mellow, gentle, leisurely, disillusioned and somewhat weary cities of the Old South getting in the game. Let one instance suffice. It is a queer sight to see Charleston, the *grande dame* of American cities if ever there was one, stirring her stumps. Nevertheless, Charleston is taking long strides beneath her hoop skirts. She has a Committee of Three Hundred, businessmen led by a radio station owner, whose announced aim in life is "More Payrolls for Charleston." Now, they boast, Charleston is manufacturing quite a number of things, from "fine trousers" to fountain pens, from "walk-in" refrigerators to venetian blinds, from steel chairs to caskets. It would be enough to warm Henry W. Grady's heart. But the smokestacks do not encroach on the Batt'ry or the gardens, and old Charlestonians speak to visitors of these newfangled things as "curiosities."

While most of the new industry in the South is small or middle-sized, some of it is big stuff by national standards, such as Kaiser's $150,000,000 basic aluminum plant at New Orleans or General Electric's $200,000,000 appliance manufacturing plant near Louisville, Kentucky, which has had to build a small city for its 16,000 workers and their families.

### From Plantation to Plutonium

These things, however, are piddling projects carried out with chicken-feed funds compared with the biggest manufacturing project ever carried on anywhere. This is the Atomic Energy Commission's Savannah River project, which is located in the fields and forests about midway between Aiken, South Carolina and Savannah, Georgia, to make a fissionable materials for A-bombs and H-bombs. The project, according to its information director, George H. Robinson, will cover 315 square miles, or an area 50 per cent bigger than Chicago; up to the middle of 1953 more than 120,000 persons had been working on it; the dirt dug for it would form a wall from New York to Los Angeles seven feet high and four feet thick; its cost will run to at least $1,400,000,000, which is some 50 per cent more dollars than were deposited in all the banks of South Carolina during 1950.

I visited the project in the spring of 1952 on my way from Aiken, South Carolina to Athens, Georgia. In the atomic no-man's land between the two, houses for workers were going up like popcorn in a hopper, and all the trailers in the world were holding a convention.

I drove to the Administration building, marched boldly up to a beautiful young woman at the information desk, told her I was a newspaperman and casually asked her if she minded if I looked around. She requested the story of my life in a few words, sent my name in to Mr. Robinson and asked me to have a seat. I watched the employees going back and forth; they were stopped by pistol-packing guards when they went from one room to another until the guards could ascertain whether their photographs on their lapels matched their physiognomies. Incidentally, these employees made up as intelligent-looking an aggregation as I ever saw, and if the girls had been chosen on the theory that in the course of human events the atomic race might at any time turn into a beauty contest, they couldn't have looked any better.

The public relations director chatted with me for a while, as with one of the taxpaying stockholders of his corporation, then lent me a car and a guide—a young ex-flier and journalism student—to take me over the place, or as much as I should see.

It was all perfectly safe. The whole thing was as much a mystery to me in the end as it was at the beginning. I saw a vast amount of construction; I saw the village of Ellenton being moved corporately down the road and out of the reservation, and finally I saw, at the heart of the project, the thing I had seen pictures of in the newspapers—a row of what looked like slenderized smokestacks or emaciated silos, giving the impression of a gigantic but ragged piece of fence in a vast, open field.

The secrets of The Bomb, from *A* to *H,* were safe with me. However, it is no secret that the Savannah River project will make no bombs of any sort, but will make the bomb ingredients which may either blow civilization to bits or lift it to heights of unimagined achievement. It will make hundreds of chemical elements which do not now exist, except by transmutation. One of these is tritium, from which the heavy hydrogen of the H-bomb is produced, and which so far costs about half a billion dollars a pound to make. What miracles of transmutation may be wrought at Savannah River no one knows, but some of the things which the AEC envisions coming out of the strange, new building blocks are radiography, atomic sterilization of foods and drugs, new species of growing things, little power plants which one can carry around with him, and the opening of new fields of knowledge in chemistry and biology.

The atomic projects in South Carolina, Tennessee and Kentucky are not industrial plants in any ordinary sense of the word, but they are having a profound effect on the South's economy today and will have a profounder one on the world's tomorrow.

## Why Does Industry Move South?

Why is industry coming to the South from other regions? What trends are discernible? Why is established industry in the South expanding so rapidly?

One obvious part of the answer is that industry is expanding in the nation and overflowing old bounds.

But that is not all of the answer by any means. The profit fields really are greener on the Southern side of the fence. The rate of industrial growth is most rapid in the South. Why?

There is a three-*M* answer to this—Men, Materials and Markets.

The National Planning Committee in a pamphlet entitled *Industry Comes South* puts it this way: "The South attracted an increasing share of the new expansion because its markets were growing faster, its supply of available raw materials was greater, and its labor supply was more plentiful than in other parts of the country."

The most important of these factors appears to be labor. The rest of the nation is learning with some astonishment that labor in the South is as steady, hard-working and efficient as can be found elsewhere. Its "on the job" record is excellent. North Carolina is not backward in pointing out that manufacturers from here and there have volunteered the opinion that workers in that state are "among the finest they have ever employed."

The South lays stress on the fact that its workers are "native-born." North Carolina claims that 99.6 per cent of its are, and South Carolina tops this with a claim of 99.7 per cent. Col. Elliott White Springs, textile manufacturer of Lancaster, South Carolina, says of his workers and their ancestors:

"They fought with Braddock on the Monongahela; they killed Ferguson at King's Mountain; they went with their Cousin Andrew Jackson to New Orleans; they went to Mexico for Cousin James K. Polk; they flung the gauntlet at Cousin Abe Lincoln, and they refused to be reconstructed by Cousin Andrew Johnson; they joined their North Carolina and Tennessee cousins in the Thirtieth Division to break the Hindenburg Line; they saddled Halsey's white horse at Tokyo; and they are ready to take on Joe Stalin or any one else who attempts to exploit them. Every spinner could be a Colonial Dame, a D.A.R., or a U.D.C., if she wished."

What's more, they turn out the goods.

There is a differential in wages, North and South; in 1952 in the textile business it amounted to about twenty cents an hour, straight time exclusive of fringe benefits. But this difference in pay is only one of many elements of costs and profits; it is not the most important one. There was a time when industry chose the South because of its "cheap labor supply." Today labor's efficiency, coupled with labor-saving devices, is more important than labor's cheapness. There is more profit in a Southern textile worker handling twelve looms at $1.23 an hour than in a New England worker handling six looms at $1.43 an hour, and this is what has been happening. The six extra looms are more important than the two dimes. Manuafcturers are looking for a steady supply of labor, low turnover, low absenteeism and satisfactory worker attitudes, and they are finding them in the South.

Accessibility to raw materials is also important to some industries. A tobacco factory, for example, locates in North Carolina to be near its materials, a cotton mill in South Carolina, a plant to make newsprint from pine trees in Alabama. It is more economical to get your raw materials next door. Therefore, pulp mills, steel mills, chemical plants, oil refineries, food processing industries and so on, are coming South.

Markets furnish the third compelling reason for the movement of industry to the South. Wages and profits flow from labor and materials; thus new markets are created. In the South of half a century ago a vicious circle existed: no production, no money, no markets. Today the circle is no longer vicious but beneficent. It is a circle of wages, production, profits and markets. Commerce follows the dollar as well as the flag. So giants in the field of distribution follow giants in the field of production, and head South.

But where is industry going in the South? Is any pattern discernible? The latest trend seems to be for industry to skip over the more industrialized areas and seek out the less industrialized ones. The hypothesis suggested by Calvin B. Hoover and B. U. Ratchford in their *Economic Resources and Policies of the South* is that whereas there was a tendency of industry to seek industrialized areas in the South between 1929 and 1939, that trend may have been stopped or reversed after 1939.

If such is the trend, why is it? Various answers suggest themselves. Management may find more labor available in rural or semi-rural areas than in overindustrialized ones. A factory in a field surrounded by a network of roads may attract workers from a considerable territory, and these workers may be more energetic and tractable than their city counterparts. There will be room to expand, and taxes and traffic will be lighter than in town. Whatever the reasons, industry is decentralizing itself in the South at top speed.

All of the Southern states are up to their necks in the business of luring new industry their way. They want to get more taxpayers instead of having to raise taxes to meet the ever increasing demands on state and local governments. "If a hunter wants to shoot birds," says Louis W. Bishop, director of the South Carolina Research, Planning and Development Board, "he can get 'em by planting peas in a field. If a state wants industry, it can get it the same way."

The most spectacular example of "pea-planting" is Mississippi's BAWI, or Balance Agriculture With Industry, program. A state law provides that any Mississippi town or district can construct housing for desirable industries and finance it with a public bond issue which must be approved by a state board. The corporation then agrees to rent the property for a certain time at a certain rental, with an option to stay on at a nominal rent for additional terms. A new company can get tax exemptions from ad valorem taxes for five years, except on its manufactured products. The site and building are owned by the municipality and so are not taxable. Thus Mississippi subsidizes new industry. This has been assailed as unfair competition by other states, both North and South, but Mississippi says BAWI is there to stay because it brings in the industry the state so desperately needs.

Special inducements to new industry are no rarity in the South. Most of the states use some form of tax exemptions or concession as a "pea field."

State advertising is another approach; it may be direct solicitation of a particular industry with migration on its mind, or it may be general. Each Southern state gets out a beautiful picture booklet telling of that state's scenic, cultural and economic advantages over the other forty-seven states; most of it is expertly designed to move the non-Southern industrialist, who is in outer darkness trying to carry on business under difficulties on a scrap of underprivileged earth, to become "a brother of the old wild goose" and start honking toward the particular "Southern part of heaven" described in the booklet.

Arkansas promoter Ham Moses unconsciously spoke for all the other Southern states when he said, "We've got to outplan, outthink and outwork all the other states if we are to maintain the pace of industrial growth we've set in the past decade."

Whether the South can keep up the pace is a question depending on many factors, some variable and others unknowable. But the trend is fairly predictable. From its present position the South will push on to the next stage in its economic life. This will be, as Professor B. U. Ratchford of Duke University predicts, a "more complex stage of industrial development," requiring "more skill and training of the workers, more capital for equipment, and management of a higher order of ability." More complex industries, such as chemicals, paper, machinery and electronics, will bring in higher wages and bigger profits. They will require of management more expertness in engineering, finance, personnel and marketing; research and designing will play a more important part in the economy. And all this will call for many auxiliary services necessary to the functioning of a complex industrial system, such as "the foundries, the industrial architects, the accounting firms, the specialized financial and legal services, the plants to use by-products, the plants to make and service machinery and equipment, the advertising and marketing agenices, and a host of others." These are the "housekeeping" services of modern industrialism which may employ more workers than the industries they serve.

The South's industrialization is just beginning.

# 6

## What You Don't Know Will Hurt You

---

Research!

It is the most important word in the South today. It is putting brawn in the service of brain at tremendous profit. It is turning old telephone poles into paper, making dollars grow on old-field pines, and any day now it will be changing sows' ears into silk purses and thistles into figs.

Research is the modern philosopher's stone which turns all it touches into gold. The South is rich, fallow and virgin —well, demi-virgin—soil for it. Research is begging the South to let it make it rich and the South is being talked into it.

In Florida materials which used to be discarded in phosphate mining are being used as a source for precious uranium ore.

In Birmingham, Alabama, paper is being made from discarded telephone poles and railroad ties. The fact that 50,000,000 poles and ties are scrapped a year makes it possible to get quite a lot of paper this way.

In Virginia wallboard is being made from sawdust.

Marble dust is being used for cosmetics.

89

Waste tobacco products are being used to make insecti-
cides.

The Southern Bio-Research Laboratory predicts that Spanish moss will soon be converted into pharmaceuticals. (This
will make for a switch on the old joke about baby's spinach,
so that when Mama tells baby to take its medicine, baby can
retort, "I say it's Spanish moss, and the hell with it!")

In Texas a scientist has borrowed nature's technique of
making hail, and is manufacturing ice thirty times faster and
cheaper than it has been manufactured. Also in Texas water
is being used instead of air in tires on heavy construction
machines, thus making for "increased traction, cooler fabric
and virtual elimination of punctures due to thorns and small
nails"—and incidentally opening a new market for antifreeze
compounds. Petrochemical research is creating a new Texas.

The South is "putting waste to work."

In Florida, when citrus growers went into the canned fruit
juice business, they found themselves with mountains of
foul-smelling citrus pulp and peelings on their hands. Finally
they dumped the stuff in rented fields. Soon they found out
that cattle grazing in the fields were growing fat on the waste.
The canneries began dehydrating the pulp and peelings, and
a new cattle feed was discovered. Cattle which used to be
shipped North to be fattened are now putting on weight in
Florida. This is an example of accidental or unconscious
research.

At Oak Ridge, Tennessee and State College, Raleigh,
North Carolina, research in nuclear physics is being directed
at both pure knowledge and practical ends. In various parts
of the South a great deal of research is being directed to the
production of new fibers for textiles with exciting names such
as acrilan and vicara.

This emphasis in the South on research is a new development. For a century and half from 1792, when a Connect-

icut Yankee named Eli Whitney came South and did a piece
of research that resulted in the cotton gin, until ten years ago
the South didn't have any use for research. You couldn't
blame it much. Whitney lost his shirt trying to get his invention on the market, and the South lost its shirt after he got it
there. Whitney's gadget changed history for the South; it is
quite plausible that if there had not been a cotton gin there
never would have been a Civil War. The South might well
say with Omar the Tentmaker, "O Thou, who didst with
Pitfall and with Gin Beset the Road I was to Wander in . . ."

So for a hundred and fifty years the South looked on research with a jaundiced eye. In 1940 there weren't enough
research institutions in the Land of Cotton to shake a tobacco
stick at.

But twelve years later there were in the South thirty-seven
research institutes, most of them run by universities. In addition there were eighteen federal research groups, some of
which worked for the armed services. And then there were
approximately forty "well-staffed and well-equipped consult-
ing industrial laboratories" where there were none a dozen
years ago.

Scientific research in chemicals is expanding faster in the
South—mainly in Texas and Louisiana—than anywhere else
in the nation.

One of the liveliest of the organizations promoting research
is the Southern Association of Science and Industry. It was
established at Mobile, Alabama in 1941 and has its headquarters at Atlanta, Georgia. Its aim is "to promote the South's
technological and industrial progress," and "to provide a
medium for the continuous co-working of industry, business
and science in making the most of the South's resources and
opportunities."

In 1948 the Southern Association of Science and Industry
started a new venture. It began publishing a scientific jour-

nal called the *Journal of Southern Research*. Some Southern industrialists declined to support it on the ground that there was not enough research news or money in the South to make a go of it. Five years later, however, the *Journal* was self-supporting, had much more material than it could publish and a circulation of over 5,000 a year. This is evidence that the South is interested in research.

President Mahlon Padget Etheredge of the Southern Association of Science and Industry notes that the Southern "industry may now obtain at nominal cost scientific advisory services in such fields as ceramics, chemical processes, electronics, food technology, metallurgy, mineral technology, sanitary engineering and textile manufacturing. . . ."

As examples of research in the South, he points out that "the Texas Engineering Experiment Station tested a new airplane designed specifically for dusting, spraying, seeding and fertilizing crops; the University of Florida reported progress in pilot plant studies of the utilization of scrub oak in paper manufacturing; Georgia Tech reported development of machines for cleaning and grading peanuts; the USDA New Orleans Laboratory began operation of a pilot plant for spinning fiber from peanut protein; the Southern Research Institute in Birmingham reported new textile treating chemicals and new derivatives of turpentine; the University of Georgia discovered methods for improving the process of canning pimientos; and a new yam variety, 'gold rush,' was reported at Louisiana State University."

North Carolina State College, in addition to atomic research, is doing a good deal of agricultural research, plant and animal genetics and soil chemistry, particularly with regard to black shank in tobacco, hybrid corn, broiler products and certified breeding of cows. It has also been working in various fields of industrial research, aiding such diverse industries as trucking, fishing, lumbering, ceramics, furniture, textiles, brick and tile. Research at this institution has perfected an adjustable gauge for furniture making by which specifications can be calculated to .001 of an inch and 8 per cent of the labor of assembling furniture can be dispensed with. Another experiment at State College indicates that North Carolina by using native clays and limestones may be able to save $8,000,000 a year on its cement bill, or at least keep that money in the state.

Yet when Dean J. H. Lampe of the School of Engineering of State College asked the 1951-52 Legislature of North Carolina for $196,000 for the biennium for research, he was promptly turned down. He will continue asking, however, in the faith that "money spent for such experimental and industrial programs in behalf of North Carolina's small industries and the development of its resources will be a real boon to our economic development."

What can research do for the South? The life of Charles Holmes Herty, who taught chemistry at the University of North Carolina at Chapel Hill before the First World War, offers two illustrations. Dr. Herty looked at the most common thing in the South—the old-field pine—and saw in it what nobody else had seen before. Industry had been killing the pines to get turpentine from them. Dr. Herty discovered that to get a good turpentine yield you don't have to cut deeply into the tree but only to the inner bark. He invented a cup to do the job. He thus not only saved untold square miles of pine forests from destruction but he also increased the yield of turpentine by 25 per cent. That's research at work.

Later Dr. Herty concluded that newsprint could be made from pine trees. Everybody said it couldn't be done—too much resin; kraft paper, yes; newsprint, no. Dr. Herty went to Savannah where kraft paper was being made from pines. He finally got the city to support a small laboratory where he could go to work on his idea. A year after his death in 1939 his idea was put to work in a newsprint-from-pine manufacturing plant at Lufkin, Texas. In 1949 the $32,000,000 Coosa River Newsprint Company, solidly based on Dr. Herty's dream, went up in Childersburg, Alabama. It is reasonably certain that other such newsprint plants will be constructed and that the South will take its place as an important supplier of newsprint to the nation. Until it does, Canadian newsprint sellers, having a virtual monopoly, can charge United States newspaper publishers what they please.

The life of Dr. George Washington Carver offers a multitude of instances of the value of research to the South. Born in Missouri during the Civil War and educated at Iowa State, he taught at Tuskegee and persuaded Southern farmers to diversify their crops by planting soil-enriching peanuts and sweet potatoes instead of cotton. When a surplus of peanuts and sweet potatoes resulted, he undertook to solve the problem of finding new uses for them. How brilliantly he succeeded is indicated by the fact that from the lowly and simple peanut he made three hundred products, including cheese, milk, flour, coffee, ink, dyes and insulating board. From the sweet potato he made, among other things, vinegar, molasses, flour and rubber. From cotton stalks he made rugs and from wood shavings synthetic marble.

## Ignorance Is Not Bliss

Why is research so important to the South? One reason is that the South has lagged so far behind the rest of the nation in this field. The South has been chronically short on inventions and patents, which are rooted in research and blossom in profits. Delaware in 1940 had 1,041 patents granted for every 100,000 of her population, whereas Mississippi had only 17. These were extreme cases, but they were sympto-

matic of what was happening in the North and not happening in the South. In 1940 Connecticut had four times as
many persons working on textile research as the whole South
had.

The South is on rock bottom in industrial research among
the regions of the country, and it is paying for it in tribute,
waste and poverty, but it is learning that it does not have to
stay there and pay. In the past decade the South has discovered that research pays handsome dividends. It has caught a
glimpse of its opportunities and is beginning to do something
about them.

But it is only beginning. Only about 5 per cent of the
industrial research is in the South. In the New York metropolitan area there are three times as many research laboratories as there are in the whole South.

Dr. Wilson Compton, president of Washington University,
put the case for research in the South powerfully when he
said:

"During the last half-century in the United States more
than one-half of our new material wealth has come from new
ideas which were not known fifty years ago, or at least were
not applied to the production of things. But for the South as
a whole, the proportion has been less than one-tenth. Rich
in diversified natural resources, the South has not been pro-
portionally rich in ideas or in opportunities . . . Of Britain
it has been said: 'Export or die!' Of the South it may equally
be said: 'Utilize, conserve and diversify—or decline!'"

The South has been living off its resources by allowing the
exploitation of its soils, forests, mines. It would be far better
if it started living off its ideas, but to do this it needs research.

If this statement needs corroboration, it may be found in
Edith Webb Williams' monograph *Research in Southern Regional Development*. The author reaches these conclusions:

The South has relatively little industrial research.

The research facilities of Southern colleges and universities are inadequate. . . . Southern students must usually go out of their region to secure the highest level of training.

The research needs of the South are so great that there is room for work by every type of agency and organization including Southern industry, business, government, colleges and universities.

The rest of the country will not wait for the South to catch up.

Harriet L. Herring, research associate of the Institute for Research in Social Science at Chapel Hill, has been stressing the need for research which would provide for fuller use of Southern resources in industrial development. Much of the South's poverty is explained by the fact that it sells its raw materials and buys them back in finished products. If the South makes sugar and peanuts, Miss Herring asks, why shouldn't it make peanut candy? The South buys a lot more candy than it makes. It might take a little research to learn to make and keep candy properly, as it does to learn to keep potato chips fresh in bags, but it pays off. The South also raises a lot of fruit, but it has lost out to other sections in the business of processed fruit because it lacks the know-how.

Miss Herring says: "The South is tired of its role as proud but poor relation to the rest of the country—the bottom of every list when strength is being counted, the top when weakness is the text. It is weary of the qualifying phrase 'below the Potomac' when any achievement is being measured. The region has long been noted for pride in its past. But this pride is stultifying without thorough self-respect in its present and buoyant faith in its future. The one can come from work well done, the other from vision made manifest."

What has been said in this chapter relates to research in the natural sciences. But research in the social sciences should not be overlooked. The University of North Carolina and the University of Virginia were the first major institutions of higher education to start research institutes in this fruitful field. From the Institute for Social Research at the University of North Carolina has poured a flood of regional analysis and interpretation, including more than a hundred published volumes and hundreds of articles and manuscripts.

The body of knowledge of the South's resources, deficiencies and opportunities resulting from such research is the firm foundation for translating the South's potential into progress. It opens up "acres of diamonds" in the South's backyard.

That is why "research" is the most important word in the South today.

# 7

## Biggest Vacation Since Crusades

---

The tourist business in the South is the biggest, richest, gaudiest and most fantastical mass vacation since the Crusades.

Nobody knows how big and rich it is. All anyone knows is that it is a multibillionaire baby. If any other business—except government—operated as haphazardly as the tourist business does, it would go broke immediately. Yet the tourist business, trade, industry, or whatever you want to call it, is too busy raking in billions of dollars to count them.

The South is selling tickets to the beauty, strangeness, romance and history which God and man gave it—from Mount Vernon to the Alamo—and it is one of the finest shows on earth.

More Yankees invade the South every year than were in Sherman's army, but now they pay their way, handsomely. They bring in, each year, more dollars than President Jeff Davis and Treasurer Christopher Gustavus Memminger ever printed.

Frank Floridians admit that they can extract money from the strangers within their gates more quickly and adroitly than the citizens of any other state in the Union. The

United States bought Florida in 1803 (it was bigger in those days) for $15,000,000, or about four cents an acre, and it was considered an extravagant price. Front footage comes higher now. Tourists now are paying close to a billion dollars a year just to visit Florida, not to buy it.

Yes, the South has a combination of romance, history, beauty and strangeness, not to mention ugliness, cussedness, poverty and problems, that lures the tourists and packs them in at anywhere from, let's say, one dollar to a hundred dollars a day.

There are said to be only five cities of unique charm in the United States—Boston, San Francisco, Charleston, New Orleans and San Antonio—and three of them are in the South.

Virginia, from Virginia Beach to the Skyline Drive, from *The Common Glory* to the Barter Theater at Abingdon, with such historic shrines as Mount Vernon, Jamestown, Yorktown, Williamsburg, Monticello and Westover, is a tourist paradise.

North Carolina, from her Outer Banks, with their history which includes such extremes as Sir Walter Raleigh's Lost Colony and the Wright brothers' first airplane, to the Blue Ridge Parkway and the Cherokee Reservation, offers attractions which tourists would not find everywhere. Some of the most beautiful mountain scenery in America is to be found in the North Carolina mountains around Cherokee, Fontana Dam, Blowing Rock, Chimney Rock, Grandfather Mountain, Mount Mitchell, the Cullasaja Gorge and the Nantahala Gorge. Pinehurst, Southern Pines and Greensboro form a kind of triple National Golf Capital, while Chapel Hill, State College and Duke constitute a triangular "intellectual capital of the South." No wonder Harold Kaplan, Jr., aged 17, wrote:

> I've never been to Timbuctoo,
> I've never been to China,
> But of all the places I've never been,
> I prefer North Carolina.

South Carolina has Columbia, Myrtle Beach and a glorious strand that stretches many miles along the coast. It has Charleston, that aristocrat of cities, and the nearby gardens of delight, Cypress, Middleton and Magnolia. There are many beautiful gardens in the world—in Japan, in China (let us hope they are still there), the Buitenzorg gardens in Java, the Versailles and Luxembourg gardens in France, the Boboli and Villa d'Este gardens in Italy—but no other garden anywhere has the colorful richness of beauty that Magnolia has.

Georgia has Atlanta with its Druid Park, Stone Mountain with Gutzon Borglum's handiwork still evident, Sea Island and Athens with its "tree that owns itself." It has many small towns with magnificent homes that were built when cotton was king.

Alabama has its lovely capitol in Montgomery—"the Cradle of the Confederacy" on Goat Hill—and its White House of the Confederacy, apparently with everything President Jefferson Davis ever owned, including the tobacco pouch which he had in prison. It has the beautiful, young, money-making city of Birmingham. It has Tuskegee. All this, and Love's Old, Sweet Song On Mobile Bay, too.

Tennessee has its TVA lakes and dams, its Hermitage, its Memphis and its mountains. It has a model tourist town if ever there was one—Gatlinburg—in the Great Smokies. There food and lodging are good even when quite reasonably priced. The tourist industry in the South ought to camp on Gatlinburg's doorsteps until it finds out how Gatlinburg does it.

Arkansas is the state of homely humor and hospitality.

When the Arkansaw Traveler played a tune on the fiddle to the Squatter's liking, the Squatter told his wife to fetch a hunk of venison from the kitchen and a jug of liquor from behind the bed. "Come in and take half a dozen cheers, Stranger," he said, "and sot down. Play away, Stranger, you kin sleep in the dry spot tonight."

There are both dry and wet spots in Arkansas nowadays, the land of honeysuckle-covered rail fences, where the White River wanders through the Ozarks. Hot Springs is a vagrant bit of metropolis set in the Ouachita Mountains. Bathhouse Row, with its establishments like Riviera casinos, hedged about with magnolias and elms, brings prize fighters, big-league baseball players, cinema celebrities to the springs to get the kinks out of their muscles and nerves.

All Kentucky is divided into three parts: the Eastern Mountains, the Blue Grass Country and Western Kentucky. Within those boundaries it has Abe Lincoln's log-cabin birthplace and My Old Kentucky Home, the Mammoth Cave and the mammoth treasure at Ft. Knox. It also has Louisville where the hotels are lined with marble. It is the land of "fine whiskey, beautiful women and the Kentucky Derby." Whether this is what Kentuckians are talking about when they say, "Heaven is a Kentucky of a place," deponent sayeth not.

Louisiana is two states in one, the northern part being predominantly "American" and Protestant, the Southern part French and Catholic. New Orleans with its old, proud and charming Creole families is the melting pot of the South and the Paris of the West.

Shaped like a boot, with its frayed heel in the Gulf of Mexico and Mississippi on its instep, Louisiana is the land of the Sugar Bowl "classic" and the Mardi Gras, the land where they bless the shrimp fleet and the sugar cane crop, the land where they celebrate Huey P. Long's birthday beneath

his twelve-foot statue near the slender, white skyscraper
capitol he built beside the bluffs of the Mississippi River.

In mansions at the ends of avenues of water oaks festooned
with Spanish moss, architects wed four-square galleries and
winding stairs to Grecian columns. The yards held *garcon-
nières* for the young bachelors, neatly balanced by *pigeon-
niers* for the doves.

Louisiana is the land where one hunts buried treasure
with the aid of a tame ghost, although the rules of the game
are rigorous, since the hunter cannot talk, smoke, drink or
"have anything to do with a woman for four days," which
may explain why so little treasure is unearthed.

New Orleans is the link not only between the old world
and the New South but also between the two Americas. In
the bad old days the planters' octoroon mistresses, beautiful
and accomplished, lived in "little houses near the ramparts,"
after arrangements had been made for them at the famous
Quadroon Ball, but they were forbidden by law to walk
abroad "in silks, jewels or plumes," lest they become too
proud and excite undue admiration in the gentlemen and
envy in the ladies.

Iniquitous and unique, New Orleans unites in itself the
massive efficiency of American commerce and the charm of
an old-world city with its filigree balconies, its half-glimpsed
patios and its reputation for fine food, fine drink and the
more alluring forms of sin.

Florida is like a green tongue lapping away at the blue sea,
or it is like a boomerang, as you choose. From ancient St.
Augustine to ultramodern Miami, it is the land of contrast
between old and new, wilderness and metropolis. You can
eat a Spanish dinner capped with a Havana cigar at Tampa,
sun yourself on the beaches at Jacksonville, enter the earthly
Valhalla of the multimillionaires at Palm Beach, or meander

with the Suwanee River under green boughs misted with Spanish moss.

But it is Miami Beach which is the main Mecca of the modern cult of sun worshippers. "The presence which rose thus so strangely beside the waters," to paraphrase something Walter Pater said of Mona Lisa, "must be what in the ways of a thousand years men have come to desire." At any rate they come from far, cold places bearing gifts, in order to see and be seen, to gaze down as paying guests, from their costly casements in the tall, white hotels, at the beach where the blue sea turns green as it meets the yellow sand. The wealth they brought built the new altars in a hurry. The island on which these hotel-cathedrals arose was no more than a mangrove wilderness, an unsuccessful coconut farm and a broken-down avocado grove as late as 1913 when John S. Collins built a bridge to it from the mainland. Forty years later it out-Babylons Babylon.

Texas, fabulous and friendly, is the only state which can, by contract with the USA, quintuple itself so as to send five sets of senators and representatives to Congress; so far, it has had the good sense not to. It is the state where the heat is hotter, the hailstones bigger and the grains of sand more numerous than in any other state.

Texas is the state which celebrates Mother-in-Law Day, a spinach festival, a rattlesnake derby, a German Saengerfest, a turkey trot, Mexican nativity plays, and a Cowboys Christmas Ball.

Its legendary hero is Pecos Bill, who must be blood brother to Paul Bunyan and at least half-brother to John Henry. Bill was brought up by coyotes; rattlesnakes ran when they heard him coming; he used mountain lions for saddle horses, and invented centipedes and tarantulas for household pets. He rode a bucking cyclone and only "got throwed" when it "rained out from under him." When his wife, Slue-Foot Sal, rode Bill's horse, "Widow Maker," he pitched her so high she had to duck for the moon, and when she landed on her steel-spring bustle she bounced back and forth so long between heaven and earth that Bill had to shoot her to keep her from starving to death.

No wonder Texas men order limousines and charge them to their hotel rooms; no wonder a Texas heiress had her day spoiled by finding a pearl in her oysters at lunch.

Texas is Houston and Dallas which have grown so rich so fast they can't count their millions. It is Randolph Field which looks from the air like a board for Chinese checkers. It is the Browning Room at Baylor University in Waco. It is El Paso with its shining roofs under the dark and crumbling face of Comanche Peak, with Mexico across the Rio Grande which is "too thin to plough and too thick to drink."

Texas is San Antonio with its Alamo, its auditorium with the tiltable floor, its downtown streets which look on the map like a "skillet of snakes," and its river which meanders through the heart of the city bearing on its banks parks, beer gardens, fountains and an outdoor theater with a water curtain. There's no place like San Antone.

Mississippi is the far-South state whose writers have exhibited the South at its charming best and ugly worst. It is the state which has the Harp Singing at Eggville, the Footwashing Services at Dennis, the Natchez pilgrimage and the Gulf Coast Azalea Trail and Festival.

The lush Delta region begins, according to David Cohn, "in the lobby of the Peabody Hotel at Memphis and ends in Catfish Row at Vicksburg."

Below it lies Natchez of the departed glory and the antique elegance, with its very old, small, town houses of severe Spanish Provincial architecture as a contrast to the luxurious, slender-columned antebellum mansions with their lovely fanlights, mosaic gallery floors, carved rosewood, gold brocade and dreaming mirrors.

And last, at the very end of the South itself, is the lotus land of Biloxi and the Gulf Coast.

## How the Millions Roll In

Few Southerners would suspect that the tourist business is the most profitable business in the South. Yet that appears to be the fact.

The South's textile industry had a profit of $2,000,000,000 in 1951, but the tourist business took in over $3,000,000,000 in that time—and most of that must have been profit.

A table of Visitor Volume and Expenditures, taken from *Americans on the Highway,* a magazine published by the American Automobile Association, gives the following estimates, in round numbers, for most of the Southern states for 1951:

| State | Number of visitors | Expenditures |
|---|---|---|
| Alabama | 2,000,000 | $40,000,000 |
| Arkansas | 6,400,000 | 197,000,000 |
| Florida | 4,800,000 | 840,000,000 |
| Georgia | 8,700,000 | 218,000,000 |
| Mississippi | 2,000,000 | 244,000,000 |
| North Carolina | 6,000,000 | 300,000,000 |
| South Carolina | — | 67,000,000 |
| Tennessee | 10,000,000 | 465,000,000 |
| Texas | 9,000,000 | 375,000,000 |
| Virginia | 35,000,000 | 468,000,000 |
| Totals | 83,900,000 | $3,214,000,000 |

These statistics should be taken with a grain of salt, because they were provided by the states "on the basis of their own research formulas," but, after making allowance for

local pride and advertising, there can be no doubt that the
tourist business in the South is astonishingly big.

Sixty million Americans take automobile vacations a year
and spend some $9,240,000,000 on them, according to the
American Automobile Association. The South, with its
beaches and mountains, certainly gets a major slice of this
vacation pie. The Blue Ridge Parkway in Virginia-North
Carolina and the Great Smoky Mountains National Park in
North Carolina-Tennessee were the two most popular areas
in the National Park Service in 1951, drawing a total of more
than 5,500,000 visitors.

What makes tourists come to a State?

Tennessee analyzes the reasons as follows:

| | |
|---|---|
| Advice of friends | 44% |
| Previous visits | 31% |
| State advertising | 17% |
| Advice of tourist bureaus | 13% |

This adds up to 105 per cent because some people come for
more than one reason. Anyway, some 30 per cent come because of state advertising plus advice of tourist bureaus which
depend largely on state advertising. Advertising evidently
pays handsome dividends.

The beauty about the tourist business from the viewpoint
of the South is that so much money comes in compared with
what goes out. Other industries manufacture raw materials
and export them at a profit. The raw material of our tourist
trade is not exportable; the tourists look at our scenery, but
they can't take it with them. Thus both raw materials and
profits remain in the state.

And yet, as we have said, the tourist industry suffers badly
from lack of organization and efficiency. What the tourist
gets for his money often depends more on luck than anything
else.

## On Treating Tourists Rough

Robert D. Calkins, director of the General Education Board, spoke the truth when he said:

"I know of no state that would not benefit from a campaign to improve and to clean up hotel and other accommodations. Every traveler complains of poor and inadequate restaurants, dirty hotels, ill-kept towns, dirty and decrepit filling stations. Many tourists are disappointed by the absence of picturesque lunchrooms specializing in choice local dishes and shops that display the best Southern products. . . . One improvement that is urgently needed is the landscaping and beautifying of the principal highways. . . . If you ever start showing off the beauties of the South, you will be astonished at the amount of beauty there is to be shown."

One can think of various things the South could do to make its already profitable tourist trade more profitable and enjoyable. For instance:

1. Get the industry better organized so it can know itself, police itself and improve itself.

2. Make a continuing study of the business and publish yearly reports. Analyses showing where tourists are going, why, how long they stay, how much they spend, how they like where they went, and so on, should be profitable.

3. Insist on better food. This applies largely to the little places—the big ones have to keep certain standards—but it is important because most people eat at the smaller and less expensive places, and a great many don't like what they get to eat. Cannot cooking schools be held for cooks who want to learn? Virginia has a "Three-C" School—courtesy, cleanliness and cooking.

4. Better lodging. A well organized industry could improve this situation.

5. More advertising on both state and local levels but much less on the billboard level.

6. More specialties, such as festivals and outdoor dramas. Several Southern states are already doing well in this respect.

7. Towns which have a good deal of charm and history could advertise themselves more and provide more and better tourist facilities.

8. State parks could be much improved with cabins and recreation facilities.

9. Highway beautification. The South has finer scenery and does a more efficient job of hiding it behind billboards, auto junk yards, snipe signs, trash heaps and so on than any other region in the Union. More turn-outs are needed where the scenery is visible so the tourist can take time to enjoy it.

### Tourists Must Eat

Tourists must eat. The tourist industry ought to pay more attention to the sort of food it serves them.

In a famous Southern seaport I failed to find any good food. The famous restaurant I ate at was so crowded that it took about three hours to get and eat dinner—and then the deviled crabs were cold and dry.

In a Virginia town I wanted to get lunch and asked a bystander where was the best place to eat. He recommended a hole-in-the-wall place. I was standing beside a nice-looking hotel and I said, "How about that?" "No," he said, "that's where they feed the civic clubs." He was right; it was no good.

In a town in Georgia I tried to find a good place to eat and spend the night. It was a charming looking town—magnificent old homes and all that. A filling station attendant told me the best place was a motor court. I went to it. The sockless proprietor showed me a rickety cabin with furniture in it that looked as if it had come from a dime store a generation ago. Then I looked over the two hotels and they were worse than the motor court. So I marched on through Georgia.

In a North Carolina resort town everybody admitted that there was no good place to eat except in the summer. I admitted it, too, after trying a couple of places including the main hotel.

In another mountain resort town the big hotels were closed, so I tried a café and ordered a club sandwich. It had rat cheese instead of bacon and the chicken meat in it had never been anywhere near a chicken breast, yet it cost seventy-five cents. Tourists don't forget meals like that. For every tourist that eats at a big resort hotel, twenty eat at a little café.

Tourists must eat. But a lot of people who run tourist businesses haven't found it out yet. It reminds me of a sign I once saw in a Durham, North Carolina hotel room, "Why Not Try Our Dining Room Before Going Out To Eat?" and of the sign in a Virginia café which read: "For Our Customers Our Best Is None Too Good."

# 8

## There's Where the Cattle, Cotton, Corn and Taters Grow

Where Cotton was King, Cow is Queen.

That is the most significant trend in present-day agriculture in the South. The South's agricultural revolution is as real as its industrial revolution.

"Green Pastures" in the South today is more than a play on words. In a fifteen-year period the South has increased its improved pasture land by 45,000,000 acres. More than that, it has 40,000,000 additional acres well adapted for pastures, which is twice as much as the rest of the country has.

And the South is doing something about it. Every Southern state is carrying on "a vigorous and intensive livestock improvement campaign."

Texas is the biggest cattle raising state in the Union. It also has one-fourth of the nation's sheep and nearly all of its goat population. Out in those wide open spaces an average-sized ranch is some 6,000 acres, while the fabulous King Ranch comprises close to a million acres. In such circumstances it must be easier to grow cattle than it is to fence them in. Anyway, Texas' cattle population increased by more than 1,000,000 head in the past five years.

Cattle marketings in Florida went up 366 per cent in a decade. Florida, Texas and other Southern states have been using imagination, too. For their hot climate they have brought in humpbacked Brahman cattle which thrive as well in the South as they do in India, though, to be sure, they have lost caste and gained weight by mixture with numerous other breeds, since the first Brahman bull came to the New World over a century ago.

Of the eighteen biggest milk-producing states in the Union the South contributes five—Texas, Kentucky, Tennessee, Oklahoma and Virginia.

### *Pasture Boom*

But other Southern states are getting in on the pasture boom in a big way, notably Mississippi, Georgia, Alabama and Louisiana. North and South Carolina have their eyes pretty rigidly fixed on cash crops, especially their "golden weed," tobacco, but they are increasing their pasture land, too.

How account for the livestock revolution in the South?

Much of it is due to the federal soil conservation practices, the work of state agricultural colleges, and pure-blood cattle associations; much is due to the work of pioneer promoters such as Seaman A. Knapp and Hugh McRae who said, "The South will come into its own when its fields are green in winter"; and much is due to the continuing efforts of enthusiasts like Dr. Clarence Poe, editor of *The Progressive Farmer,* and Dean Paul Chapman of the University of Georgia.

They have been preaching the gospel of livestock production as a balancing influence for cash crops, to the tune of

Iago's "put money in thy purse," and Southern farmers, who
have no actual distaste for the long green money from the
long green pastures, have harkened to their preaching. Now
pasture crops such as lespedeza, fescues, Ladino clover and
kudzu from the Orient, make better pastures possible.

Dr. Poe in particular has used *The Progressive Farmer* as
a pulpit for this message. "The South," says he, "can and
should become one of the great livestock, dairy and poultry
regions of America." He draws word pictures of "millions of
Western cattle and sheep freezing and starving in snowy bliz-
zards" while "here in our sunny South contented cows were
grazing on green pastures which had not been snow-covered
all winter." He quotes Louis Bromfield and others to the
effect that the South can produce milk and beef on its own
ground more cheaply and profitably than they can be produced in the Middle West.

This combined appeal to sentiment and pocketbook, kind
hearts and staggering profits, has touched many a Southern
farmer's better self and moved him to add cattle to crops.

What true Southerner could be averse to rescuing those
pitiful calves and lambs from Northern ice and snow as long
as steaks and chops bring what might be conservatively called
"a pretty penny" a pound on the market?

Nor is it calculated to discourage the agrarian descendants
of the men who followed Lee and Jackson to read in a Federal Reserve Bank of Richmond booklet "The Story of How
A North Carolina Farmer Made Himself A $10,000 A Year
Man" and "increased his net worth from $2,830 to $23,080
by switching from cotton to cows."

Poultry raising is another phase of animal husbandry which
is big, new and pleasantly profitable business in the changing
South. Thar's gold in them biddies, suh.

If you throw in Maryland and Delaware (which ought not to be too hard to throw) the South produces practically all of the nation's supply of "fried chicken." In 1934 Georgia sold about $200,000 worth of these friers, in 1950 over $50,-000,000 worth. Georgia is now close to being the Chicken Capital of the USA. Other big producing states are Arkansas, Virginia, Texas and Alabama.

All this—and country hams, too!

### Yes, We Have Crops

It may be spectacular to watch the South changing to a region of livestockholders, but don't forget that it raises crops also.

In 1950 it raised nearly $5,000,000,000 worth compared with some $3,000,000,000 worth of livestock and livestock products. Of the crop money, cotton accounted for slightly over $2,000,000,000, and tobacco for a little more than $800,000,000. North Carolina is the biggest tobacco-growing state, with Kentucky the runner-up. In the Fifth Federal Reserve District, which comprises Maryland, West Virginia, Virginia, North Carolina and South Carolina, for every dollar brought in by livestock, two dollars were brought in by crops and one of those two was a tobacco dollar. North Carolina and the Federal Government did not object.

### Wealth in Wood

Another crop of immense and growing value to the South is its timber crop.

The South has the largest and fastest growing forest area in the nation—2,000,000 acres.

In the old days timber sold for little or nothing; trees that took centuries to grow went for two or three dollars an acre. But not now. Ask the man who owns one. Ask the man who has tried to buy a plank lately, but don't ask the man who has tried to buy a home, because he may shoot you. Timber nowadays seems not far from the price range of semiprecious stones.

The reason is that while there is plenty of demand for wood for its old uses, such as for poles, ties, construction, furniture, and so on, research has provided many new uses for old-field pines, oaks, poplars, gums, et cetera. Pulpwood is a relatively new commodity. Clothes, plastics, newsprint and multitudes of other things are made of it. Pulpwood sales have been going up like the latest-model jet fighter plane, from 460,000 standard cords in 1929 to 10,000,000 in 1950.

Thus while the South is increasing the profits it gets from its cash crops—ranging from cotton to peanuts, and from rice to oranges—it is adding wealth from timber and from live-stock including cattle, sheep, goats, horses, poultry and—oh, yes—chinchillas.

In the decade from 1940 to 1950 the South, i.e., the rural South, made greater gains than any other part of the country in electrification, telephones, tractors, motor trucks and auto-mobiles. On the Southern farm the mule is giving way to mechanization, ignorance to research, and Tobacco Road to civilization.

A. L. M. Wiggins, of Hartsville, South Carolina, former president of the American Bankers Association, was talking sense when he told a conference of Georgia bankers:

Here in the South we stand in the midst of vast undeveloped resources—economic possibilities as yet largely untouched. It is as if we were lulled by the sound of a mighty waterfall but have not harnessed its energies. Here we have the climate, the sunshine, the rainfall, the soil and the people, the bountiful blessings of Almighty God, and—for the first time in our history—a substantial amount of liquid wealth, all beckoning us to a future unlimited for ourselves and for the generations that come after us.

# 9

## "Take Two and Butter 'Em While They're Hot"

---

When purple twilight fills the South
  With silver sound of supper bell
And in the oven's sooty mouth
  Hot rolls in golden glory dwell,
When grace is mumbled and the guests
  Have all been helped to chicken breasts,
Now when the rolls are served you'll hear
  The homefolks say, as like as not,
Words welcome to the stranger's ear:
  "Take two and butter 'em while they're hot!"

"I haven't got a thing to eat
  But stay and take potluck with me,"
Aunt Lina says.  I grab a seat,
  Well knowing what potluck will be—
Hams and chickens, pies and steaks,
  Tomatoes, potatoes, chocolate cakes,
And glorious, burnished, glowing rolls.
  "I love to see you eat a lot.
Here, child, are some right off the coals,
  Take two and butter 'em while they're hot!"

116

Though Poverty so long has been,
 My South, your house's lord and master,
Though your once lovely face is thin
 And hardened by an old disaster,
Yet your brave gaiety and pride,
 Your generous ways have never died;
Hellenic hospitality,
 The courtesy of Camelot
Survive in your fair words for me,
 "Take two and butter 'em while they're hot!"

O Prince, for whose Satanic state
 I am, I fear, a candidate,
I'll bet my head, nor fear to risk its
 Brains, that when you serve your dinner
And imps bring in your brimstone biscuits,
 You'll hear some gracious Southern sinner
Say to the rest of the blazing lot,
 "Take two and butter 'em while they're hot!"

Most Southern cooking is bad. A good meal is hard to find; you always get the other kind.

But there are three sorts of Southern cooking which are good. They are:

1. Outdoor or folk cookery
2. Amateur or home cookery
3. Professional or New Orleans creole cookery

Travelers in the South who have heard of the delights of Southern cuisine are about as likely to find them as they are to be hit by a meteor—unless they have some Southern cousins or belong to a Southern country Sunday school.

This explains why tourists get a shock when they cross the Mason-Dixon line and gleefully enter a café rubbing their hands and licking their chops with the thought: "Now for some real Southern fried chicken!" Just why they think they will find that *rara avis* in a restaurant, of all places, is still a mystery to Southerners who have been trained to look for it only at home.

As they travel over the South their disappointment increases and they write feelingly of "the starchy, monotonous, porcine, heavy and overdone motif in the cooking, done-to-death fried chicken, hominy grits" in the form of "a mess of pure white gunk with a small pool of gravy cupped in it," overcooked and greasy vegetables "like mildewed dishrags," pot likker which tastes "as if the cook had forgotten to empty the dishpan," and so on.

But there are notable exceptions. There are oases in the Sahara of Cuisine.

There are people in the South who know how to baste bluefish with butter so that it need not fear comparison with Antoine's *pompano en papillote,* who know how to cure hams over hickory smoke that would make a Hammus Alabammus fancier turn green with envy, who can do things with shrimps and crabs that are not to be spoken of but with bowed heads, and who can prepare barbecue (if given twenty-four hours) that bears the same resemblance to the wayside Bar-B-Q product that a Beethoven violin concerto does to a Crosby croon.

## Folk Cookery

The first great branch of Southern cooking includes the brunswick stew, barbecue, fish fry and Sunday school picnic. The brunswick stew and barbecue go together; the other two are strictly separate and distinct.

The scene of the barbecue is an oak grove on a hill; the stage properties are a big iron pot in which the brunswick stew is simmering and a pit in which the pig is being roasted over embers. The dramatis personae are a score of men. The

time is sunset. Not a soul can be seen. The reason for this
is that everybody is at the spring which is below the brow
of the hill.

The spring supplies the chasers. In the old days of prohibition the drink was corn liquor. Sometimes it was a light
amber color if it has been kept for a while in a charred (or
"charged") keg, but mostly it was as innocently colorless as
water and as powerful as Niagara. The accepted drinking
procedure was to pour the corn from a five-gallon jug into a
glass by inserting the index finger in the handle of jug and
elevating the bottom of the jug on the elbow above the shoulder so that the liquor would run freely. This did not make
for exact measurement, nor was that the object of the game.
A man would pour a generous amount of corn into his glass,
add water to it from the spring, glance sideways at the fusel
oil and maybe a stray mosquito floating on the surface of the
concoction, shudder, raise the glass with a convulsive motion, down the drink, gag, gasp, regain breath and swear, "By
God—boys, that's the f-f-f-finest—drink I ever t-t-t-tasted!"

Today the drink is bourbon and branch water—a more
civilized but not such a quick-acting drink. Bourbon taps
you with boxing gloves; corn slugged you with brass
knucks.

But what of it? *Hilaritas Sapientiae et Bonae Vitae Proles,*
as the Founding Fathers used to say when young at the Raleigh Tavern in Williamsburg. A few shots of corn or bourbon awaken the appetite and prepare one for the first course,
which is the brunswick stew. This is served back in the oak
grove from the big iron pot by means of a long-handled ladle
wielded by an old Negro. The stew is poured or rather
shoveled into boat-shaped receptacles made of very thin wood
—or used to be before wood got so scarce.

A good brunswick stew is made of practically everything
on the farm and in the woods, including chickens, beef, veal,

squirrels, okra, beans, corn, potatoes, tomatoes, butter-beans, vinegar, celery, catsup, sugar, mustard and enough red pepper to bring tears to your eyes. With it go slices of light bread, ready for dunking if you like it that way.

A variation of brunswick stew is Kentucky burgoo. Or perhaps it would be more accurate to say that burgoo is the ancestor; at least some Kentuckians claim that burgoo was the mess of pottage for which Esau sold his birthright. The original recipe for burgoo started off with "800 pounds of lean beef with no bones or fat"—but why go on?

If the stew dulls your appetite, it had better go back to the spring for resharpening, because the best is yet to come.

All this time the pig over the coals has been gradually readying himself for his barbecue apotheosis.

In fact he has been unwittingly preparing for this moment all his life. This is no ordinary pig of the stockyards but a sacrificial pig, young, tender, innocent, virginal, which Uncle David, ancient High Priest of Barbecue, has nurtured from its birth almost as a member of the family. No exercise has marred this pig's flesh; no cares have fused their acids in its capillaries.

This morning at sunrise Uncle David slit Pig's throat, in a dedicated manner, dressed Pig, cut off its head and split it down its belly. At noon he laid the victim face downward and spread-eagled on chicken wire over a pit filled with oak embers. For seven hours Pig has been cooking. Every now and then little drops of grease fall into the embers with a slight spitting sound. A delicate and entrancing odor rises from the almost imperceptible smoke and is wafted towards the road so that

From Piggy's buried ashes such a snare
Of barbecue is flung into the air
That not one true believer passing by
But shall be overtaken unaware.

During the cooking Uncle David has replenished the embers continually and has turned Pig over so that its skin side is roasted too. Many times he has basted Pig with a mixture of vinegar, red pepper and salt by means of the simple and humble apparatus of a rag tied to the end of a stick so that finally the sauce has become incarnate in Pig.

Not until Pig's fat is crackling crisp is the cooking complete. That explains why barbecue cannot be transported or warmed over but must be eaten on the spot; the contrasting textures of soft flesh and crisp fat are essential. When they are right, the result is heavenly.

With the barbecue go white bread and corn bread to absorb the sharpness of the vinegar in the sauce, and water and cole slaw to mitigate the red pepper. Little wooden spoons and forks are frequently provided, but barbecue tastes best when eaten with the fingers.

Another traditional form of Southern folk cuisine is the fish fry. Roark Bradford gives a celestial version of one in the opening of *The Green Pastures*. It is an ancient feast, going back to Palestine.

Something new, however, has been added in the South—the hush-puppy. These are golden-brown dabs of fried corn meal. The name originated, according to legend, when the cook at a fish fry threw a handful or two of corn-bread batter into the deep fat the fish had been cooked in, and then hollered "Hush, puppies!" in order to quiet the dogs which had gathered around and knew a good thing when they smelled one.

The Sunday school picnic is more refined than the barbecue or the fish fry. The food varies a good deal because each family brings what it makes. Not every family has a good cook in it, but quite a few do, and it is a matter of pride to send to the picnic the best, or anyway the almost best. By picking and choosing one can find very good food. I speak from experience here. "Myself when young did eagerly frequent" these outings. Whenever I got wind of a picnic in prospect (and it was a source of suspicion of Providence on my part in my early days that the Episcopal church to which I belonged had few, if any, picnics compared with the Methodist and Baptist churches) I immediately and shamelessly repaired my friendships with the boys (and even girls) of the church which was planning a picnic, and sometimes went so far as to pump the church organ in order to wangle an invitation.

It was worth it to me when I finally got to the rustic tables in the country churchyard, covered with fried chicken, slices of old country ham, beaten biscuits, buttermilk biscuits, rolls, deviled eggs, pickled peaches, watermelon rind pickles, sausages, lemon pies, chocolate pies, apples pies, peach pies, pecan pies, blueberry pies, chess pies, coconut pies, black bottom pies, potato salad, sliced tomatoes, chocolate cakes, Lady Baltimore cakes, caramel cakes, devil's food cakes, angel cakes, scripture cakes, and so on and so on. One of the most baffling experiences of my life was to eat all I could possibly hold and then discover, too late, a chocolate layer cake (theretofore somehow hidden from my eyes) of a supernatural softness, lightness, beauty and fragrance, about which I could do nothing.

I understand precisely what Chancellor Robert B. House of the University of North Carolina at Chapel Hill means when he says that as a boy he attended so many "big meetings" with "dinner on the grounds" that when he eats a piece of fried chicken today the act is automatically followed by a "conviction of sin."

### Slightly Savage

This outdoor Southern cooking for hungry people springs from an ancient tradition. Indeed it goes back to the Indians and what they taught the lost colonists on Roanoke Island and the more durable colonists at Jamestown. The Indians knew tricks about food that meant the difference between life and death to English settlers in a strange land. There were no cows in this country in the early days of its settlement; many a white child was brought up on hickory nut "milk," which consisted of the kernels beaten to a milky pulp, because that was what many Indian children were nurtured on.

The debt Southern cooking owes the Indian is set out by Silas Spitzer in *Holiday* magazine:

"The prehistoric Indians of the South were the great cooks of their time. The streams and lakes swarmed with fish, wild fowl darkened the skies or glided down to feed in the marshes. Thousands of wild turkeys made the dawn ring with their gobbling shout. Many weighed fifty pounds and stood taller than three feet. We are told that some of the Virginia colonists used thick slices of the white breast meat instead of bread. Nowhere did nature smile more pleasantly on the occasional labors of a lazy man.

"The Indians' supreme gift to civilization was corn. The rich soil produced heavy ears of delicious sweetness. And soon Southern settlers learned the exquisite new joy of devouring young green corn that had been freshly boiled or roasted in the hot coals. They ate corn hulled, pounded and ground; or stewed with beans, deermeat and black-bear fat in a hefty and succulent version of what we now call succotash. Sweetened with wild honey or maple sugar, it was often steamed in puddings. The squaws ground the fat white kernels with beans and potatoes and patted this flour into

thin cakes, or kneaded corn meal in rough loaves that came
out brown crusted and smoking hot from a rude earthen pot
buried in the glowing heart of an open fire.

"The Indians taught the impoverished gentlemen of the
Jamestown Colony how to cook the odd-looking but tender
and juicy opossum in a nest of honey-sweet yams; how to bake
doves and quail and partridge in a blanket of wet clay, and
dined them nobly on acorn-fed wild boar and venison. The
accommodating tribesmen showed them how to catch huge,
lazy catfish with their bare hands.

"An early colonist wrote that, in the tidal waters along the
coast, he came upon 'whole bancks of oysters and scallops . . .
which made sweet breakfast eating.' The Englishmen had
never seen anything like these American oysters, which were
often thirteen inches long, broad as a man's hand, and amaz-
ingly fat. A curious touch is that many of the more epicurean
natives smoked oysters over fires of green wood, exactly like
the cocktail tidbits that are served at parties nowadays."

All this is in the higher reaches of folk cookery of the
South. When you get into the lower reaches you run into
possum and 'taters, and when you get down to rock bottom
there are chit'lins.

A possum (or opossum if you want to get technical) is a
nocturnal and omnivorous animal with a reputation for fre-
quenting graveyards. For this and other reasons, many people
with strong imaginations and weak stomachs won't eat possum. On the other hand, lots of people like him very much.
If you ever want to cook one, Silas Nicholson of Southern
Pines tells how in Bill Sharpe's *State Magazine* (Raleigh,
North Carolina):

"All you do is put the 'possum in an open baking pan
(same one you used for the Thanksgiving turkey) and place
it in the oven (top part, not the broiling part) and cook at a
very low temperature until done, basting every thirty min-

utes with a barbecue sauce containing only vinegar, black pepper and plenty of red pepper.

"The reason for the red pepper is that the 'possum is very fat, and you have to have that red pepper to stimulate the digestive organs to take care of the fat, or else you will be sicker than no little.

"I believe you should warn your readers that it takes a mighty good man to eat 'possum and 'taters. In fact, chances are that if he can't drink likker from a fruit jar, he maybe should lay off 'possum and 'taters."

If you can eat possum, maybe you can eat chit'lins. Chitterlings, to get literary about it, are the small intestines of a hog, and they can smell a house up about as efficiently as a skunk can. A few hardy souls can eat them fried. Still fewer can eat them boiled—in water full of salt and red pepper— with a mess of turnip greens on the side. But most people prefer to keep a reasonable distance from them—say, a mile and a half on a still day, and double that if the breeze is blowing.

### Southern Home Cooking (Not to Be Read When Fasting or Dieting)

"Aunt Lina," said Mama, "you know the ladies didn't drink in your day!"

"Drink?" said Aunt Lina, who had been born and brought up before the war (Civil War, of course) and even before the Victorian era, "I should say they did drink. Why, every evening at the Springs the gentlemen used to send a tray of mint juleps up to the ladies in their rooms before supper."

As a matter of fact, Aunt Lina was drinking a mint julep at that instant in her room at home. It was in the early afternoon, but there was no need for hurry. Her dinners (they were not lunches) rarely started before three o'clock in the

afternoon—to give the diners time to let breakfast settle—and
it would be two-thirty anyway before the turkey would be
done properly. Violet, the colored cook, would see to that,
and after she had finished her julep Aunt Lina would go in
the kitchen and give the meal its finishing touches.

The gentlemen were having their juleps in the parlor.
These juleps had the confident simplicity of great works of
art. Violet had picked a dozen handfuls of the mint from the
mint bed between the woodhouse and the backhouse while
the dew was still on it and had kept it in the icebox. She had
cracked the ice and got out the big silver goblets rimmed
with the Greek key design. But nobody except Aunt Lina
had *made* the juleps. She had put a lump of loaf sugar in the
bottom of each goblet, dissolved it in a mite of spring water,
pressed the mint with the back of a silver spoon against the
goblet until it had yielded up its flavor, then filled the goblet
with cracked ice. The next step was to pour from a bottle of
venerable and mellow bourbon until the amber liquor
reached a hair's breadth of the top, then garnish with sprigs
of mint until one was reminded of Coleridge's words—"and
ice mast-high came floating by as green as emerald." The
result was a drink which was smooth and sharp, sweet and
biting, cold to the fingers and hot to the stomach, delicate
but authoritative, and "annihilating all that's made to a green
thought in a green shade."

"Gentlemen," said Uncle John to Papa and me, "that is
reverend stuff."

Slightly faint with hunger, a proper state for the task before us, we trooped into the dining room around three
o'clock. Aunt Lina's table was longer than most dining
rooms are nowadays. It was a sturdy mahogany board covered with a snowy cloth and it was loaded to the Plimsoll
line. At one end was a turkey and at the other a ham; in between there were foods which will be hereinafter described.

Aunt Lina presided over the turkey; Uncle John carved the ham. Aunt Lina was a vigorous old maid whose ruling passion was to watch people eat. Perhaps she got that way by feeding starving soldiers at the end of the Civil War. She had lived a long time and been through a lot; she had shopped at "old A. T. Stewart's" in New York; she had seen Lincoln—how she hated him!—ride his white horse into captured Petersburg. She thought the end of the world had come and so she moved to North Carolina. Next to Lincoln she hated President Hoover because she considered him responsible for food rationing—this was during the First World War—and she was resolved to show him he couldn't get away with any such imbecile, unconscionable and subversive trick as far as she was concerned. Uncle John, who married one of Aunt Lina's nieces, was once Aunt Lina's pride and joy because of his superhuman appetite, but now he had gotten so fat—he was about five feet, six inches tall and weighed at least 275 pounds—that he was afraid to eat as much as he used to, on account of his heart trouble. This didn't daunt Aunt Lina who continued to stuff him as much as she could, but it was rough on Uncle John because it kept him torn between love of food and fear of death.

As Aunt Lina looked over her crowd, she decided she had had better ones. Grandma and Mama and Mary (Uncle John's wife) were pretty good eaters but nothing unusual. Papa had dyspepsia and could eat very little; this kept him very mad and caused him to make invidious remarks about the other diners, such as, "I believe John and Aunt Lina could eat a bushel of buttered bricks between them." The children and Jim and I saved the day, however. When Aunt Lina cast her eyes on us, she knew we would do our duty. The stomachs of soldiers and children, as she knew by experience, are almost bottomless.

Aunt Lina spread out her hands, closed her eyes, bowed

her head and said grace. At first I was afraid she would say
the one she used to tell us as a joke:

> Down on your knees and up with your paws
> And thank the good Lord for the use of your jaws.

But she used the regular one, about "make us thankful for
these and all Thy blessings." Sometimes she put in something about "make us mindful of the needs of others," which
occasionally came out "make us needful of the minds of
others," but this time she cut grace short to get down to
business.

Aunt Lina carved the turkey. It was a noble bird, a not
unworthy descendant of the wild turkeys of the early American wilderness which stood three feet tall and weighed up to
fifty pounds. This one weighed some thirty pounds and his
oven-tanned figure had been cooked from shortly after dawn
to a little after 2:00 P.M.

Aunt Lina loaded ivory white slices of turkey breast onto
our plates and accompanied them with spoonfuls of dressing
—compounded of bread crumbs fried in butter, chopped turkey liver, chopped and fried onions, corn bread to give it the
right texture, sage, parsley, salt, pepper and Lynnhaven oysters. All was christened with golden turkey giblet gravy.

Uncle John carved the ham. The thirty-pound miniature
mountain which rose before him like a sand dune at Hatteras
was no ordinary ham. True, the hog was not peanut-fed; it
grew to maturity on nothing more recondite than slops and
acorns. What then made it unique? It was cured by Mr.
R. E. Lee Davis, who was an artist. If he were a painter or a
sculptor he would have signed this masterpiece.

Three years ago he trimmed it and cured it over hickory
chips and a sassafras twig or two, *con amore.* Then he coated
it lavishly with a combination of salt and black pepper and
hung it up to age in his smokehouse. When it came to Aunt

Lina's hands a few days ago it had attained that perfection which only time can give to old wine, old cheese, old violins and old friends.

It was then a dark and unappetizing looking monstrosity. Violet, however, knew what to do. She washed it in hot water scrubbing off the salt and pepper with a stiff brush, then soaked it over night in cold water to prevent it from being too salty. Next day she boiled it very slowly and carefully, seeing to it that the water merely simmered and none of its *elan vital* boiled off. When done (you can tell when the little bone in the hock, not the big one, comes loose), she let it cool in the water it was cooked in, then took it out, cut off the tough outer skin and covered the pearly fat with a mixture of bread crumbs and brown sugar moistened with sherry. Cloves could do nothing for such a ham but get in the way. Then she baked it—but only long enough to caramelize the sugar.

So it came to the table; Uncle John lifted his carving knife and sliced through the brown integument and the nacreous, translucent fat to the dark and rosy meat beneath, spangled here and there with little white specks which are the hall-mark of the well-cured country ham. "A ham," said Uncle John, "should be as spicy as a woman's tongue, as sweet as her kiss and as tender as her love."

At the sight and smell of Mr. Davis' masterpiece, the heart of the carver leapt up and the hearts of the diners with it. Such hams are the immediate jewels of the connoisseur's soul. Like a Stradivarius or a Vermeer, they are where you find them; they are not mass-produced, they are not on the market. There are other good hams in the world, but the hams of Wiltshire, Westphalia, Czechoslovakia and Smithfield cannot compare with this one. There are reports that the hams of Estramadura alone come close to it in quality. One whose palate had once appreciated this ham would no more eat a

midwestern American commercial ham than he would pull
a shingle off the roof and devour it. It has the combination
of strength and sweetness hardly to be found outside the
verses of Lucretius and Chaucer, the paintings of Rubens and
Michelangelo, the music of Mozart and Beethoven.

This is a vintage ham which must be masticated with meditation, savored with joy and remembered with thanksgiving.
As Uncle John carves it, a look of lustfulness comes over his
countenance such as must have been imprinted on Tarquin's
face when he gazed on Lucretia in her bed.

It is the "ham what am" or rather the "ham what was,"
because the curing of such hams has become by the year 1953
A.D., a lost art, like the making of stained glass for cathedral
windows in the Middle Ages. This art was never widespread.
It existed only in the Old South and in very few parts of
that; for example, it flourished in eastern North Carolina
and Virginia, skipped over the Piedmont and the mountains,
but arose again phoenix-like in middle Tennessee and in
Kentucky. "I often wonder" what these ham artists buy
"one-half so precious as the stuff they sell." They must have
got to wondering about that, too, because they don't sell the
great, old, three-year hams any more—except perhaps to a
handful of lifelong friends—but put on the market hams
which have been given a lick and a promise of curing for a
year or less and which are only a degree or so above packers'
hams.

The ham and the breast of the turkey complemented each
other from their ends of the table like a violin and a harpsi-
chord.

Is there any bread to go with this combination of white
and red, dull and sharp? Well yes. There are:

Beaten biscuits, small, thin, crisp and marked in the center
with nine fork dents forming a little square;

Rolls puffed with pride and burnished with butter;

Sally Lunn, sweet and gentle;

Eggbread, served with a spoon;

Popovers, or muffins which have exploded, leaving their insides a nonentity and their outsides crisp as a cracker;

Corn bread, which Violet confidentially tells guests her people can't eat because it "scratches their throats"—an infallible but imaginary sign of superaristocracy.

Any vegetables? A few. For instance:

Butter beans, small, tender, verdant, dusted with black pepper and gilded with butter;

Crimson beets humid with vinegar;

Light brown corn pudding, with the fresh, sweet ivory-colored kernels of the corn baked in eggs, cream, butter and flour;

Deep-emerald turnip greens;

Potato pancakes, brown and round with lacy edges;

Sweet potato soufflé in orange baskets;

But, no grits. Aunt Lina remembers a soldier telling her in 1864: "All I've had to eat for years, lady, is grits, grits, grits. I'd just as soon lie down and let the moon shine in my mouth."

Salads? No room for such.

Desserts? We have to make room for these:

Ambrosia—golden orange slices like crescent suns on a snowy bank of coconut blushing with sherry;

Tipsy cake, first cousin of the "Tipsy Parson" so called because it formed part of the traditional feast when the preacher came to dinner. It is a gigantic sponge cake baptized with scuppernong wine, covered with custard, surmounted with syllabub and topped with blanched almonds.

Then, at twilight, cigars and stories. "I love a good cigar," said Aunt Lina, meaning that she liked the smell of one because it reminded her of the good old days at the "fashionable wat'ring places," before Victoria and Lincoln and Jeff Davis and Sherman and Grant ruined the world, when the brandy came from France, the carpets from Brussels, the cigars and rum from Havana, the diamond shirt studs and the servants from Africa, and the gentlemen from the South.

## A Little Breakfast

Let us not overlook the old-timey Southern breakfast. It is an institution—perhaps the best loved meal of the region— at any rate, for people who have gone to bed early and hungry, slept the sleep of the just and risen "early on a frosty morning."

For this breakfast there are no fripperies and no preliminaries—no juice or melon or cereal. You plunge directly *in medias res* which being translated means old country ham, chicken, bacon and sausages, salt herring roes, rolls, toast, biscuits, waffles, coffee and—never to be forgotten—buckwheat cakes.

These buckwheat cakes are not the "plate o' w'eats" of the North shored up with puny sausage links. They are not the product of the ready-made "mix" which comes from a pasteboard box with indecent haste and moves without meditation or art from carton to griddle.

This rare species requires long training—such as Violet has had—with nothing to disturb the equanimity of the artist, and careful preparation the night before when the ingredients ("magruduses" to Violet), including 'east cake, potato water, white flour and dark, water-ground buckwheat flour, are beaten up and left behind the stove in a gray earthen crock. Next morning, milk, black molasses, baking powder, soda and a "fraction" of salt are added. Indeed all the "magruduses" are measured in "fraction." Nobody knows what a "fraction" is. This art is not for the books.

But when the cakes come off the griddle they are too good to have their taste adulterated by any sort of syrup. Serve a stack topped by a stick of butter and accompanied by a few slices of strong, old country ham or equally strong salt herring roe mashed up in butter, and you have a dish which will make lunch, or even dinner, a work of supererogation.

There is something Gargantuan about Southern cooking. Tom Wolfe got at it in *Look Homeward, Angel* when he wrote of his own family:

"They fed stupendously. Eugene began to observe the food and the seasons. In the autumn they barreled huge, frosty apples in the cellar. Gant bought whole hogs from the butcher, returning home early to salt them, wearing a long work-apron and rolling his sleeves half up his lean, hairy arms. Smoked bacons hung in the pantry, the great bins were full of flour, the dark recessed shelves groaned with preserved cherries, peaches, plums, quinces, apples, pears . . .

"In the morning they rose in a house pungent with breakfast cookery and they sat at a smoking table loaded with brains and eggs, ham, hot biscuits, fried apples seething in their gummed syrups, honey, golden butter, fried steaks, scalding coffee. Or there were stacked batter-cakes, rum-colored molasses, fragrant brown sausages, a bowl of wet cherries, plums, fat, juicy bacon, jam. At the midday meal they ate heavily: a huge, hot roast of beef, fat, buttered lima beans, tender corn smoking on the cob, thick red slabs of sliced tomatoes, rough savory spinach, hot yellow corn bread, flaky biscuits, deep-dished peach and apple cobbler spiced with cinnamon, tender cabbage, deep glass dishes piled with preserved fruits—cherries, pears, peaches. At night they might eat fried steak, hot squares of grits fried in egg and butter, pork chops, fish, young fried chicken."

## New Orleans Creole Cookery

This is the third great branch of Southern cooking. Unlike the Southern folk and home cookery, it is more exquisite than Gargantuan, more professional than amateur. Self-conscious and sophisticated, it demands a "fine seriousness" in its practice and is a business which comes as close to being an art as anything can which does not convey meaning but only gives pleasure.

In New Orleans the tourist comes upon cooking which is the equal, if not the superior, of any in the world. He may be tempted to say that it is not Southern or American cooking at all but continental or cosmopolitan.

However, if he does say so he would be wrong. It is Southern cooking, but with much borrowed here and there from many parts of the world—France, Spain, Massachusetts, Virginia, and Africa.

Those who have never eaten New Orleans oysters Rockefeller, crawfish bisque, crabs timbale, gumbo file, *pompano en papillote,* pommes soufflés, and crepes suzette, for instance, have something to live for; those who have eaten them have something to go back for.

It so happened that the first time I saw New Orleans, it was a memorable day. It was in fact the historic date in the First World War when national prohibition went into effect.

It hit New Orleans like an earthquake, typhoon or other act of God. People were pouring all sorts of wines, whiskies, brandies, gins and liqueurs into the gutters. What a time!

What a place! What gutters! Canal Street lived up to its name that day.

About twilight I came upon a quiet and slightly antiquated restaurant which looked strangely—miraculously—familiar to me although I had never been in New Orleans before; I went in and the sense of recognition deepened. It was Antoine's. I had recognized it from reading about it in one of O. Henry's stories, and it was wonderful.

But New Orleans has its folk cookery as well as its *haute cuisine*. For instance, there is the "Po' Boy Sandwich." It consists of a long, crisp loaf of French bread (a *"flute"*) hollowed out in compartments, which are filled with various meats such as ham, chicken salad and sausage. The name comes from the story that a generous merchant in the French Market used to give them to little Negroes who called to him, "Mistah, please give po' boy a sandwich." This is what is called "a snack" in New Orleans to distinguish it from a meal.

Another name for it, or something similar to it, is "La Médiatrice" ("The Peacemaker"), which is a loaf stuffed with butter and fried oysters, very hot. New Orleans husbands are said to take it to their wives as a peace offering when they (the husbands) come home perilously late.

Certainly the "Po' Boy Sandwich," alias "La Médiatrice," sounds as if it must have originated in New Orleans. But not so. There is plenary evidence that it goes back to England. E. Smith's *Compleat Housewife*, London, 1739, gives this recipe for Oyster Loaves:

Take a Quart of middling Oyſters, and waſh them in their own Liquor; then ſtrain them through a Flannel, and put them on the Fire to warm; then take three quarters of a Pint of Gravy and put to the Oyſters, with a Blade of Mace, a little white Pepper, a little Horſe-raddiſh and a Piece of lean Bacon, and half a Lemon; then ſtew them leiſurely. Take three Penny Loaves, and pick out the Crumb clean; then take a Pound of Butter, and ſet on the Fire in a Sauce-pan that will hold the Loaves, and when it is melted, take it off the Fire, and let ſettle; then pour off the Clear, and ſet it on the Fire again with the Loaves in it, and turn them about till you find them criſp; then put a Pound of Butter in a Frying-pan, and with a Dredging Box duſt it with

Flower till you find it of a reaſonable Thickneſs, then mix that
and the Oyſters together; and when ſtewed enough take out the
Bacon, and put the Oyſters into the Loaves; then put them into
a Diſh, and garniſh the Loaves with the Oyſters you cannot get
in, and with Slices of Lemon; and when you have thickened the
Liquor, ſqueeze in Lemon to your Taſte; or you may fry the
Oyſters with Batter to garniſh the Loaves.

Thus it appears that Southern cooking is various in its
origin. The Williamsburg art of cookery got as far South as
New Orleans, enriching, by the way, home cooking in most
of the South. And while English cooking, after benefiting
from a seachange, was spreading southward, Spanish-Mexican
cooking was infiltrating northward by way of Texas and
Louisiana.

As Southern cooking came from many lands, so it has gone
to many lands. One of the most interesting examples of its
transplantation is Liberia. A "Sometime Resident of Liberia" writes in the Baltimore Evening Sun:

"Few Americans realize that only in these Liberian house-
holds does the traditional cooking of the old American South
still prevail in all its glory. The table groans under such deli-
cacies as crab gumbo and oysters Charleston compounded of
rice, chicken, green peppers, saffron and many other good
things, which are served in Liberia in all their rich variety.

"Unforgettable too are the many hot breads and biscuits.
Sally Lunn (still called Sally Lunn) is made in Liberia with
'rising' as in the old antebellum days . . .

"In Liberia homes you will find a sumptuous array of old-
fashioned American cakes . . .

"Their most fabulous is watermelon cake. The interior is
colored pink with rose extract and dotted with black currants
or raisins; on the outside is a pale green icing made from
pistachio nuts.

"One Liberian housewife—and I hope she is still plying her

art—knew how to mottle the icing with two different shades of green in order to make her cakes look like Georgian watermelons."

Evidently our soldiers will little note nor long remember what they did in Liberia, but they can never forget what they ate there.

"Joy is one of the duties of life," as the authors of the *Gourmet's Guide to New Orleans* so wisely put it. It is a truly Southern sentiment. But so is General Lee's dictum that "Duty is the sublimest word in the English language."

So it is the South's sublime duty to eat, drink and be merry as long as the food and drink hold out. It would take an ancient Greek or a Han-dynasty Chinaman to think of anything better.

# 10

## What's All the Shooting About?

The South, according to crime statistics, is the most violent part of the country, by far. The statistics show that Southerners assault, maim and murder one another at a rate which is far in excess of that of any other region, and with a profusion, indifference and abandon which are unique. Why?

Tell this to the average Southerner and he will not believe you; cite him the figures and he will contend that there is something wrong with them. "Don't bother about the statistics," he will say, "but look at the people. Did you ever see any more kindly, easy-going, courteous and gentle folks in your life?"

He has a point there, too. But the statistics won't budge. Nevertheless, the average Southerner doesn't live in fear of meeting a violent end any more than the average Northerner does. Experience has taught him that he is in no appreciable danger.

A Northerner, relying on the crime statistics, might be pardoned for concluding that if he took a tour of the South, he would stand a very good chance of getting cut, shot, maimed or murdered before he got much farther south than Raleigh. But the fact is that he would be quite safe (except, of course, on the highways). Southerners don't waste their violence on strangers; they reserve it for their friends and relatives.

Conversely, a Southerner, contemplating a tour abroad from the port of New York, might be excused for believing, from the news of crime by Sing Sing graduates on the New York waterfront, that he would be in grave peril of life or limb on his progress from taxi to gangplank. In fact, he would be quite safe. The waterfront gangsters reserve their violence for one another. It is a strictly business proposition; liquidations are limited to crooks who get out of line by trying to muscle in on the other fellow's bailiwick, or hijack a load of furs which some other racketeer has already hijacked, or engage in some other business practices which the underworld looks on as unfair or indiscreet.

The point is that violence, North or South, is not indiscriminate, but is on the contrary limited to a certain cast of characters. If you are not in the dramatis personae, you stand very little chance of getting hurt—except, of course, by an automobile or an act of God, which might happen to you anywhere.

It is hard to believe that homefolks are dangerous; it is easy to believe that "furriners" are. My thirteen-year-old daughter Katherine, who lives in Greensboro, North Carolina, and who is a television crime-show fan, naturally looks on New York City as the crime capital of the country and is anxious to go there to see in person what the shooting is all about. When I tell her that New York is a relatively peaceful place, but that she lives in the most violent, lawless and dangerous section of the country, she simply does not believe me; she looks at me as if I were trying to do her out of a promised trip to New York or fix it so that the visit would lose its savor. "You wouldn't let me go out alone at night in New York," she says, and I have to admit that I wouldn't.

Doubtless these are natural human reactions. A Southerner would wander on the back streets of Charlotte, North Carolina or Birmingham, Alabama, both cities with high standing in murder statistics, without fear at all hours, but if he found himself on a dark side street in Chicago, New York, Boston or even Providence, he would shake in his boots and call for the police.

This rule of psychology works backward as well as forward. While I was stationed at a camp in Mississippi during the First World War, I received in the middle of the night a company of men from various Northern cities. They were the scrapings of the manpower barrel; it was the roughest, toughest, meanest, scurviest bunch of men I had ever seen assembled in one place; it was, and is, my firm conviction that they were impressed into the service from the lowest and most vicious criminal joints and dives in the country. The officer who brought them said, "Sign here for 250 men," and I counted them and signed, although I was certain that at least half of them would be AWOL by morning and that I would be court-martialed for losing them. But not at all. Next morning and thereafter they were all there. Why? Because they were scared to put a foot beyond the confines of the camp and into the *terra incognita* of the Mississippi hinterland. These metropolitan desperadoes would no more have ventured into that undiscovered country in the dark than they would have voluntarily jumped into a lion's den or snake pit. We fear the strange, the unknown.

With this introduction, let us consider the rates of certain crimes of violence in the South as compared with other parts of the nation.

Here are the urban rates for non-negligent homicide per 100,000 population for the several regions, as compiled by the Federal Bureau of Investigation in its *Uniform Crime Reports* for the years 1942 to 1952, inclusive:

| Year | New Eng. | Mid. Atl. | E.N. Central | W.N. Central | S. Atl. | E.S. Central | W.S. Central | Mt. | Pac. |
|---|---|---|---|---|---|---|---|---|---|
| 1942 | 1.3 | 2.9 | 4.2 | 3.3 | 15.5 | 19.7 | 12.8 | 3.8 | 3.9 |
| 1943 | 0.9 | 2.5 | 3.8 | 3.1 | 12.5 | 14.8 | 12.3 | 4.5 | 3.9 |
| 1944 | 1.2 | 2.4 | 3.9 | 3.1 | 13.1 | 15.2 | 11.3 | 3 | 5.4 |
| 1945 | 1.2 | 2.9 | 4.5 | 3.3 | 13.9 | 16.9 | 12.8 | 4.1 | 5.5 |
| 1946 | 1.5 | 3.6 | 5 | 4.8 | 15.9 | 19.4 | 15.9 | 5.6 | 5.9 |
| 1947 | 1.4 | 3.4 | 4.9 | 4.2 | 14.3 | 18.7 | 14.1 | 4.7 | 6.3 |
| 1948 | 1.4 | 3.4 | 5.3 | 4.3 | 13.8 | 19 | 12.7 | 4.8 | 4.6 |
| 1949 | 1.2 | 2.7 | 5.1 | 3.3 | 13.4 | 15 | 12.4 | 5 | 4.7 |
| 1950 | 1.1 | 2.6 | 4.2 | 3.7 | 10.9 | 14.4 | 9.5 | 3.1 | 3.1 |
| 1951 | 1.2 | 2.5 | 4.3 | 3.1 | 10.3 | 12.4 | 9.1 | 2.7 | 3.2 |
| 1952 | 1.09 | 2.8 | 4.5 | 3.9 | 10.4 | 12.3 | 10.6 | 3.6 | 3.3 |

In this table the New England states are Maine, New Hampshire, Vermont, Massachusetts, Rhode Island and Connecticut.

The Middle Atlantic states are New York, New Jersey and Pennsylvania.

The East North Central are Ohio, Indiana, Illinois, Michigan and Wisconsin.

The West North Central are Minnesota, Iowa, Missouri, North Dakota, South Dakota, Nebraska and Kansas.

The South Atlantic are District of Columbia, Delaware, Maryland, Virginia, West Virginia, North Carolina, South Carolina, Georgia and Florida.

The East South Central are Kentucky, Tennessee, Alabama and Mississippi.

The West South Central are Arkansas, Louisiana, Oklahoma and Texas.

The Mountain states are Montana, Idaho, Wyoming, Colorado, New Mexico, Arizona, Utah and Nevada.

The Pacific states are Washington, Oregon and California.

It will be noted from these figures that the homicide rate in the South (including the Southwest) is, roughly speaking, nearly ten times that of New England and three or four times the rates of the other sections.

Now let us look at aggravated assaults. This crime as described in the *Uniform Crime Reports* "includes assaults
with intent to kill; assault by shooting, cutting, stabbing,
maiming, poisoning, scalding, or by the use of acids. Does
not include simple assault, assault and battery, fighting, et
cetera."

Here are the figures from the *Uniform Crime Reports* on
aggravated assaults for four sections, per 100,000 population,
for the years 1942-1952 inclusive:

AGGRAVATED ASSAULTS

| Year | New Eng. | Mid. Atl. | S. Atl. | E. S. Central |
|------|----------|-----------|---------|---------------|
| 1942 | 9 | 31.2 | 178 | 147 |
| 1943 | 10.9 | 28.6 | 159 | 105 |
| 1944 | 9.9 | 28.9 | 180 | 133 |
| 1945 | 12.8 | 31.7 | 190 | 157 |
| 1946 | 13.8 | 35.2 | 197 | 180 |
| 1947 | 12.2 | 37.5 | 231 | 181 |
| 1948 | 13.2 | 34.6 | 253 | 164 |
| 1949 | 11.7 | 31.7 | 253 | 153 |
| 1950 | 11.7 | 35.4 | 218 | 119 |
| 1951 | 12.1 | 34 | 214 | 102 |
| 1952 | 13.4 | 61 | 233 | 106 * |

* I have left off the decimals in the South Atlantic and East South Central states figures. There seems little use in bothering with fractions of
homicides when killings run over 100.

The *Uniform Crime Reports,* as far as I know, furnish the
most helpful and reliable crime statistics we have on a national scale, but how useful they may be for comparing one
area with another is questionable. The FBI merely acts as a
clearinghouse; it gathers crime statistics from various local
officials and does not vouch for their accuracy, although it
does try to check on them, at least to the extent of seeing
that they are not patently out of line with known facts. It

warns users of its *Reports* against drawing conclusions from comparisons of crime data from different communities, because of the multiplicity of factors affecting crime, reported or unreported, in any given community.

That this warning should be taken seriously is indicated by the fact that, from 1949 through 1951, the crime data (at least in burglaries and robberies) furnished the FBI by the New York City Police Department were so obviously false that the FBI refused to include them in its *Uniform Crime Reports* for that period. For the first six months of 1948, New York City reported only 1,498 burglaries and 848 robberies, whereas for the first six months of 1952 it reported 21,678 burglaries and 4,469 robberies. The number of these crimes did not rise that fast; the police evidently were not reporting properly from 1948 to 1952.

In Chicago in 1951 about 97 per cent of the burglaries and 91 per cent of the robberies did not result in indictments.

Such situations as have occurred in New York and Chicago do not make crime any less in the South, but if these and other states, in which police departments were under pressure to make a good showing by sweeping crime under the carpet, would report accurately, the South might look a little brighter by contrast.

Nevertheless, the *Uniform Crime Reports* are the best, if not the only statistics, we have in many fields of crime. The FBI does an excellent job of gathering them, considering the means at its disposal. Perhaps it should have wider power to see to it that local reports are at least honest.

### Certain Questions

Certain questions raise themselves:
What part of the South's violence is Negro violence?

How much does availability of weapons, such as guns and knives, have to do with Southern violence?

How much does the traditional Southern code of honor have to do with it?

The Southeast boasts the highest proportion of Anglo-Saxon blood; why are Anglo-Saxons so law-abiding in Britain and so violent over here?

Does climate have anything to do with Southern violence?

How do patterns of violence differ, North and South?

## Negro Violence

Certainly an important question has to do with the racial distribution of crimes of violence. Do crimes of violence committed by Negroes raise the South's rate materially from what it would be otherwise? The answer is: Yes.

Racial differences in homicide rates in the South for 1940 are shown in the following table prepared by the National Office of Vital Statistics (based on rates per 100,000 population of the same race groups):

| State | White | All Other Races |
|---|---|---|
| Georgia | 5.6 | 47.1 |
| North Carolina | 4 | 28.3 |
| South Carolina | 5 | 24 |
| Virginia | 5 | 27.2 |
| Alabama | 6.9 | 34.4 |
| Kentucky | 10.4 | 61.6 |
| Tennessee | 7.1 | 61.5 |

Since practically all persons of the "all other races" in these Southern states are Negroes, the Negro homicide rate in 1940 was roughly from about five to ten times white rates.

Similar evidence may be adduced on the national scale. Arrests in the nation for criminal homicides for the five years,

1947-51, are listed by race in the *Uniform Crime Reports* of
the FBI as follows:

| Year | White | Negro |
|------|-------|-------|
| 1947 | 3,555 | 2,959 |
| 1948 | 3,579 | 3,072 |
| 1949 | 3,456 | 2,918 |
| 1950 | 3,372 | 2,899 |
| 1951 | 3,407 | 3,029 |

From the same source, arrests for assaults are given as follows:

| Year | White | Negro |
|------|-------|-------|
| 1947 | 31,863 | 25,759 |
| 1948 | 31,025 | 26,780 |
| 1949 | 31,577 | 26,769 |
| 1950 | 31,277 | 27,619 |
| 1951 | 31,963 | 28,933 |

The *Uniform Crime Reports* for 1952 show the following
racial proportions of arrests for the following crimes of violence in 232 cities over 25,000 in population:

*Murder and Non-negligent Manslaughter*

| Whites | Negroes |
|--------|---------|
| 444 | 829 |

*Aggravated Assault*

| Whites | Negroes |
|--------|---------|
| 4,270 | 7,555 |

The total number of whites in these cities was 808,357 and
the total number of Negroes 281,442.

In view of the fact that Negroes are approximately one-
tenth of the population of the United States, it is evident
that their proportion of such crimes of violence is far in
excess of the proportion they bear to the total population.

And if what applies to the nation applies to the South, it is evident that the fact that the South leads the nation in crimes of violence is largely accounted for by the very high rate of Negro violence.

Not altogether, however; if the Afro-Saxon population of the South is unusually violent, the Anglo-Saxon population is pretty violent, too.

It is interesting to note that arrests of Chinese in the nation per 100,000, according to the *Uniform Crime Reports,* never amounted to as much as ten in criminal homicide or as much as fifty in assaults in any year from 1942 to 1951, inclusive. Arrests of Japanese for these crimes was substantially less than arrests of Chinese in that period.

Sociologists have been careful to point out that the Negro's high rate of crimes of violence does not mean that he is by nature more criminal than the white man; indeed, it is hard to see how he could be. It does mean, however, that the Negro is very largely responsible for the pre-eminent position which the South holds in such crime rates. Charlotte, North Carolina, from 1940 to 1952 had an average of twenty-six killings a year, in twenty-two of which Negroes were involved.

In justice it should be pointed out that the education and training of Negroes are less than those of whites, their poverty greater, their housing conditions worse; that they are often in a new and strange environment, especially in the cities of the North and West; that they are frequently abused by the police and sometimes by the courts.

Several factors should be noted:

1. Negro violence in the South is generally confined to the Negro race. There is little violence between whites and Negroes. Negroes in the South maim and murder one another with an indifference which is shocking and at a rate which is unique. The violence which the white man inflicts on the

Negro is, as some Negro leaders recognize, insignificant compared with the violence which Negroes inflict on one another. Anything which can be done to reduce violence in the South will help the Negro most.

Why there is little interracial violence in the South is no mystery. A white man cannot beat up a Negro one day and expect him, or any other Negro, to work for him the next; furthermore, he might get beat up himself or get "in trouble" with the law. A Negro cannot assault a white man—much less a white woman—without grave danger to himself from the white people and the white courts. Thus interracial violence is too dangerous to the participants, and the community in which they live, to be indulged in to any considerable extent. Since the races have to live together in the South, they have made mutual accommodations; each race has tended to conform to the other's ways. It is no more than would be expected of human beings who prefer to take the path of least resistance and who have no desire to make their lives "nasty, brutish and short" by daily bickering and fighting—lurid fiction and Communist propaganda to the contrary notwithstanding.

2. Negro violence in the South is generally confined to the lower class. Upper-class Negroes probably indulge in crimes of violence little, if any, more than the upper-class whites do.

3. The most striking thing about Negro violence is the triviality of its causes. (The same thing applies to much of the violence by whites in the South, also.) Fights which turn out to be fatal often start over such things as a dog, a pint of corn liquor, a whore, a crap game, the meaning of a verse in the Bible, and so on. A man cuts another for not telling him when the next bus is due; a husband shoots his wife for asking him for a dollar; a wife stabs her husband because of some argument—and cannot remember what they were arguing about.

Frequently violence occurs because somebody is bored; he is reduced to breaking the monotony of life with a little melodrama; in other words, he is determined to "raise hell and put a chunk under it." When I inherited my father's law practice, I inherited the criminal law business of a Negro family by the name of Hawkins. Uncle Twitty Hawkins, the patriarch of the family, was sanctimonious in appearance, with his mahogany skin and white goatee, but he was as addicted to violence as any of his numerous sons were. Known as "good Negroes" as far as the white folks were concerned, they were continually "in trouble" with the law because of their affrays with other Negroes. Their favorite weapons were switch-blade knives and a "blued-steel," family pistol. Finally Uncle Twitty concluded, sensibly enough, that he would save money if he could get his family's legal work done wholesale. Life for him and his family was fun, but it was expensive. He had heard of a retainer fee. So he came to my office one day and inquired, "Lawyer, don't you want me to pay you an entertainer fee?"

I had not realized before how much of the violence of the South arises from sheer boredom and is classified in the minds of those who perpetrate it as entertainment—entertainment not merely in some of the phases of violence but in all of them, from the violent act itself to the "day in court," with all the dramatic possibilities inherent in the administration of Southern justice.

3. The Negro's environment, according to the sociologists, has a strong causal connection with his crimes of violence. "The position of the Negro in American society," says Dr. Guy B. Johnson of the University of North Carolina, "with all this means in terms of subordination, economic insecurity, and incomplete participation enters significantly into every aspect of Negro crime causation." Certainly it enters into some, such as robbery and prostitution, and probably it

enters into all. But while it is easy to see how poverty and frustration might lead a Negro to rob or steal from one better off than himself, it is not so easy to see why they should lead him to maim or murder one who is in the same boat with him.

The truth is that violence committed by Negroes is too often excused or explained away by sociologists; it is looked on too lightly both by Negroes themselves and by the white courts.

At first thought it would seem that stiffer sentences by the court would tend to reduce this violence, but on second thought it would appear that a defendant would rarely have as much to fear from the court as he would from the fight which he starts or willingly enters. Whether harsher court action would do much good is problematical. But if it did it is certain that Negroes themselves would benefit greatly by the reduction of violence in the South.

### The Family Shotgun

How much does availability of weapons, such as guns and knives, contribute to the South's violence? The answer is: a lot.

"High Court To Hear Seven Murder Cases" was the headline in a Wilson, North Carolina newspaper. It was a modest headline because there was nothing particularly unusual about it. The news story started off as follows:

"Charles Bethea is only one of seven persons who will face murder charges when the criminal term of Wilson Superior Court opens Monday."

The story was accompanied by a picture of Bethea, a young Negro man with fun-loving eyes and a mouth parted in a smile resembling half a watermelon—the face of a man who was patently easy-going, indolent and good-natured. The news story continued:

"Bethea is a Wilson colored man who was arrested by local police officers shortly after he fired a shotgun blast into the forehead of another colored man, Hilliard Farmer."

Just a run-of-the-mill case.

What of the other six cases on the Wilson docket? "In the seven murder cases . . . three of the victims were killed by shotguns, three with knives and one with a foreign-made pistol."

A typical criminal docket.

Shotguns and knives are not standard equipment for people in urban, industrial or commercial centers in the North, but they are for people in a rural or semirural environment in the South. Shotguns are used for hunting, and knives have a multitude of uses on the farm. Nearly every house in the countryside will have at least one shotgun and a number of knives in it.

So it happens in the South that many tussles, squabbles or arguments which begin in fun end in death. When tempers rise and deadly weapons are handy, there is a dangerous situation. What would be fist fights in Maine are knife fights in Georgia. In a Negro graveyard in South Carolina there is said to be a tombstone with this inscription: "He fought the good fight, but his razor was dull."

What can be done about it in the South? It is a very difficult problem. Shotguns, rifles and knives are not only weapons, they are also indispensable instruments on the farm. The state could not forbid and perhaps could not even license their possession. Police officers could not search persons indiscriminately to see whether they had knives on them.

Something might be accomplished by the courts giving more severe sentences to persons caught using, or about to use, knives or guns on their fellows.

But fundamentally the best hope is in the spread of education and civilization.

## What Code of Honor?

How much does the Southern code of honor, the tradition of avenging insult with injury or death, have to do with the South's standing in crimes of violence?

Practically nothing. Probably not as much as would be represented by a small fraction of one percentage point in homicide and assault rates. Such crimes in the New South are as rare as they are spectacular.

The class of people who commit the overwhelming bulk of the crimes of violence in the South today wouldn't know a code of honor if they met it in the road, and if they ever recognized it they would have no more use for it than Falstaff had.

Once upon a time, of course, things were different. The Old South of a century ago prized a code of honor which made murder practically mandatory if a gentleman or a lady —especially a lady—were insulted. But that was a matter solely for the upper classes. Gen. Thomas Jefferson Green in the good old days gave his son "a brace of dueling pistols" on his twenty-first birthday, but one would hate to think what a mother would do to a husband who made such a gift nowadays.

The books and records of the South certainly used to be replete with honor killings.

The life and death of Col. W. C. Falkner, grandfather of novelist William Faulkner, present a revealing example of violence in the old and deep South, not so very long ago, under the so-called code of honor. For forty years (from 1849 to 1899) in Mississippi attempts were made on Colonel

Falkner's life which were as consistent as they were irrational, and which ended only when Colonel Falkner did.

Colonel Falkner was a lawyer, a railroad builder, a colonel in the Confederate Army, and the author of a novel called *The White Rose of Memphis*. He was not a typical Southerner, being realistic rather than romantic, and peaceful rather than pugnacious, and he was in the end the victim of that violence in which he did not believe. The bare facts of his life, as told by Robert Cantwell, are stranger than any fiction his gifted grandson ever wrote.

In 1849, W. C. Falkner was suddenly attacked by one of his best friends, Robert Hindman, who aimed a pistol at Falkner's chest from two feet away and pulled the trigger three times. Each time it snapped. On the third try Falkner pulled a knife from his pocket and stabbed Hindman fatally.

Why did Hindman try to kill Falkner? It is said that Hindman had been proposed for membership in a "secret temperance society" to which Falkner belonged and that Falkner spoke in behalf of Hindman's acceptance, but that Hindman was told that Falkner had opposed him. There was also evidence that Falkner had, as a young man, angered several Mississippi men of prominence because he had written the life of an atrocious murderer named McCannon, whom he had saved from a mob bent on lynching, and in the course of the narrative mentioned various persons with whom McCannon had been friendly in his earlier days. These persons accused Falkner of insulting them by associating their names with McCannon's, but whether this had anything to do with Robert Hindman's attempt (or later attempts by other persons) to kill Falkner is not known.

Falkner was tried for the murder of Robert Hindman, Thomas Hindman, brother of Robert, acting as prosecutor. Falkner was acquitted on the grounds of self-defense. As he left the courthouse, Falkner was attacked by Thomas Hindman and while defending himself he killed a man named Morris who had entered the fight on Hindman's side. Falkner was tried for the murder of Morris and was again acquitted.

After this second trial Thomas Hindman tried to shoot Falkner again, this time across a dining room table, but it happened that the pistol fell from Hindman's hand and the shot went over Falkner's head. Falkner then drew his own pistol and prevented Hindman from recovering his weapon but did not attempt to harm Hindman. Hindman then challenged Falkner to a duel. Falkner accepted but set out such extravagant terms as to reduce the proposed duel to an absurdity. Friends succeeded in preventing the duel and Hindman left the state.

In 1889, Colonel Falkner, while unarmed and engaged in a business conversation on the street, was shot and killed by another friend, J. H. Thurmond, without apparent cause. After being shot he turned to Thurmond and said, "Dick, what did you do it for?" Then he died.

But all that was over fifty years ago. The good old days are gone in the land of cotton.

Killings because of outraged honor may still occur in the South, but they are only a drop in the manslaughter bucket. Perhaps a few fathers or husbands enforce the unwritten law with the family Smith and Wesson, but only a very few. Certainly it is safer to have a smiling acquaintance with a Southerner if you call him a "bastard" or a "son of a bitch," but these are not the fighting words they used to be in the South before most Southerners got used to such appellations as terms of endearment in Uncle Sam's army.

No, explanation of the stratospheric heights to which Southern criminal violence rises must be sought in something besides honor.

## Anglo-Saxons, Tame and Wild

Does history help explain Southern violence? The South boasts that it has the highest percentage of Anglo-Saxon blood in the United States. Both North Carolina and South Carolina make claims that 99 per cent of their population is of Anglo-Saxon (this includes Afro-Saxon) extraction. Yet both these states stand at or near the top in crimes of violence. Again, this raises the question: If Anglo-Saxons are so law-abiding in England, why are they so lawless in the South?

In England the railway carriages have signs forbidding passengers to put their feet on the seats in front of them. The English accept these signs as a command; Americans accept them as a challenge. The Englishman looks on the law as something to be respected; the American looks on it as something to be broken.

Yet it is clear from history that the "Anglo-Saxon" (our shorthand, catch-all word for Angles, Saxons, Jutes, Danes, Norwegians and various other "Northmen" who set up housekeeping in the British Isles after having committed all the crimes known at that time) is by nature as violent a fellow as can be found on earth. He may be tamed and domesticated, but he is naturally wild. If modern practitioners of violence, such as the Italian members of Murder, Inc., would read the early chronicles of the Northmen, such as the *Saga of Burnt Njal* or the *Song of the Volsungs and Nibelungs* (of how Hogni's heart was lifted from him, of how Gunnar was cast into the Worm-close or Snake Pit, and of how Swanhild was trodden under the hooves of horses, driven over her after she was bound "in a gate of the burg" and her face was at last covered to prevent her from frightening the horses with her eyes), the Latin hair of these latter-day mobsters would stand on end "like quills upon the fretful porcupine," at such unabashed recitals of violence for violence's sake. It is indeed, as the title of a book implies, a long way from Beowulf to Virginia Woolf.

The United States is English in origin, and as James Truslow Adams once observed, "even making allowance for the hordes of 'foreigners' who have come here, there must be some reason why today England is the most law-abiding of nations, and ourselves the least so. It is impossible to blame the situation on the foreigners. The overwhelming many of them were law-abiding in their native lands. If they became lawless here, it must be largely due to the American atmosphere and conditions."

Why so? Why is this "nation of laws, not men," the nation of the most lawless men? Students of history, of course, point out that America was settled in large part by the most adventurous, energetic, violent and criminal elements in the British Isles. H. C. Brearley in his *Homicide in the United States* notes with massive understatement that "many of the early settlers left Europe under a cloud of judicial disfavor; the disorganization of frontier life did not encourage respect for authority." And he goes on to say that "the Revolutionary War developed the doctrine of 'the right of revolution'; the expansion of the West made a hero of the desperado."

These are some of the factors making for lawlessness in America, and it is true that our heritage is a violent one, but it is certainly not more so than that of our Anglo-Saxon forebears. The evidence strongly points to the conclusion that the British are more law-abiding than we are because they have been domesticated, perhaps a thousand years, longer than we have been.

But they do not explain why the South is the most violent part of the United States. It would seem that the West should be, because the most energetic, adventurous, violent and criminal elements of American society have been going

West for a couple of hundred years or more. But compared with the South, the West is mild and tame.

Some writers blame America's lawlessness on the frontier, or at any rate the spirit of the frontier. Thus Arthur Pound in *The Sunny Side of Crime* (Independent CXVI) makes this contribution to the unraveling of the mystery:

> American crime is a cross between Original Sin and the Frontier Spirit. . . . One reason the British who stayed at home bred a peaceful posterity is that they lacked a frontier. . . .
>
> As the frontier moved west, it rolled along its load of deviltry —horse stealing, cattle rustling, murders, gang feuds, lynchings, gambling, stage-coach stickups, train robberies and bank robberies . . . That our geographical frontier has passed signifies nothing as yet; our great cities, the present hotbeds of crime, are the frontiers for a host of new Americans, offering to their released energies and stimulated wants as many immunities and opportunities as the West used to offer its "bad men."
>
> Civilization is a taming process. The British are tamer than Americans; likewise more civilized . . . The bandit is just as much a part of our social picture as the dole is of theirs.

The frontier spirit may explain American violence to a certain extent, but does it explain Southern pre-eminence in American violence?

It is not easy to see how it does. The frontier is essentially an unsettled area, a place of dynamic change with new and energetic people continually entering the scene and colliding with one another. The South is not that way at all. It is, on the contrary, an old, settled land, where the same rather easy-going people and their progenitors have lived for a long time. On the other hand the South does possess some of the qualities of the frontier; it is largely rural, it is traditionally independent, and it is historically rather weak on the organization of its forces of law and order. The frontier theory, I think, may explain some of the South's lawlessness, but not a great deal of it.

Does climate have anything to do with the South's excessive violence? It seems so.

From the *Uniform Crime Reports,* it is clear that the rates of murder and aggravated assault do go up in the hot months, down in the cold ones. As Joseph Cohen points out in the *Annals of the American Academy of Political and Social Science,* "Crimes of violence have a definitely regional distribution. The highest rates for murder and assault are found in the South. The fourteen states with the highest per capita rates . . . are grouped continuously in the southeast quarter of the country. The next group is the tier to the north which includes Pennsylvania, Ohio, Illinois, Indiana, Missouri and Kansas. New York, New Jersey and the far western states have relatively low rates. Human life is safest from homicide in New England and the northern prairie states. To a surprising extent, those states form contiguous blocks, states of nearly equal rates lying adjacently. . . ."

Throughout the country crimes against the person are more numerous in summer, those against property more numerous in the winter.

Whether warm climate makes people more bellicose may be doubted, but it is certain that it is more likely than cold climate to bring them out of their houses and onto the streets, highways and byways where they are more apt to get into fights than if they had stayed at home. This applies especially to poorer people with bad housing conditions who are responsible for most of the crimes of violence anyway. Which comes first, the chicken or the egg?

So it would not be surprising if the longer span of warm weather in the South tends to increase the rate of crimes of violence simply by giving people more opportunity to meet, mingle and maul one another, whereas the longer span of cold weather in the North has just the opposite effect. Anyway, that's the way things seem to work out; while violence is frozen in New England, it is springing up like sap in the South.

### Patterns of Violence, North and South

Patterns of violence, North and South, are quite different. As a rule violence in the North is organized, in the South spontaneous; in the North violence tends to serve gain, in the South anger. The gangs and rackets of the North from the Capone gang to Murder, Inc., are organizations which make large profits from crime and which reach their ends by corruption and violence, thus creating a situation which may be worse than violence itself.

The South has plenty of violence but it is of a different order. Organized violence is not popular or plentiful; violence in the South is often terrible, but it is not often premeditated. There is some racketeering in the larger cities, particularly in the gambling and bootlegging fields, but racketeering, with the calculated violence which goes with it, has not become generally acclimatized in the South—at least not yet. Southern violence is mostly a spur-of-the-moment, even lighthearted affair. Neither party stands to gain materially by it, and both are likely to be maimed or killed. That there is nothing calculated about most violence in the South is mutely testified to by the triviality of the causes of so much of the mayhem and murder.

The French say they do not understand Americans because over here we shoot people we haven't even met. This may be true of the North but not of the South. Down South we hardly ever shoot anybody unless he (or she) is an old friend or a member of the family.

There are—or have been—two spectacular and notorious exceptions to the general rule that Southern violence is unorganized and uncalculating: lynching and the Ku Klux Klan.

Lynching is the worst of crimes in a civilized community because it hits not only at the citizen but also at the law which protects all citizens.

But lynching has dwindled in recent years so as to be practically nonexistent in the South today.

Tell this to a European and he will be skeptical; tell it to an Asiatic and he will be certain it is a lie; even a lot of Americans might be dubious about it. Communist propaganda has made it its business to create and foster the impression throughout the world that lynchings are frequent, if not everyday occurrences, in the South. Southern fiction has helped spread this misconception by using lynchings in plots as its stock in trade. Woodrow L. Wyatt, a Labor M. P. of Britain, who made a three-months tour of the South in 1952 said: "I did not expect to find a complete reign of terror. I did not suppose that lynching was a daily routine. . . . But I did believe that the Negroes went in fear. . . . They might have been freed by Lincoln, but I thought they could not look a white man in the face." Mr. Wyatt had to change his preconceptions fast.

The fact is that there have not been as many as nine lynchings in the United States in any one year since 1936, nor as many as four in any year since 1947. Here are the statistics:

| Year | Lynchings |
|------|-----------|
| 1936 | 8 |
| 1937 | 8 |
| 1938 | 6 |
| 1939 | 3 |
| 1940 | 5 |
| 1941 | 4 |
| 1942 | 6 |

| Year | Lynchings |
|------|-----------|
| 1943 | 3 |
| 1944 | 2 |
| 1945 | 1 |
| 1946 | 6 |
| 1947 | 1 |
| 1948 | 2 |
| 1949 | 3 |
| 1950 | 2 |
| 1951 | 1 |
| 1952 | 0 |

In 1950 one of the two lynched was white, the other colored.

Of course one lynching a year is one too many, but fiction and propaganda would have a hard time existing if they had only as many lynchings in their works as the South has in real life. Nor is all this to say that there should be no federal law against lynching; perhaps there should be in case lynching ever becomes popular again, but what it does seem to prove conclusively is that for the time being lynching is not a crime which is soaring to unmanageable proportions in the South or anywhere else in the United States.

The popular conception of lynching as a Southern institution designed to "keep the Negro in his place," and to preserve the purity of Southern womanhood by terror is not quite supported by history. Lynching is said to have got its start in the 1830's with the summary execution of crooked (and, of course, white) gamblers in Virginia and Mississippi. But it must have been much older than that, say, nearly as old as the first horse thief. It was extremely popular in the West after the discovery of gold in California made that region a land of "men, not laws." In fact it followed and was part of the frontier as it advanced westward across the continent. Vigilante committees, or "popular tribunals," in California, Utah, Nevada, Oregon, Washington, Idaho, Montana, Arizona, New Mexico, Colorado and other states in their rough and early days swung thousands of men at a rope's end in application of what today would be put down in the statistics as lynch law.

In the tragic era following the Civil War, when orderly government had substantially broken down, the South did indulge in an orgy of lynching which was motivated by fear of the newly freed Negro, instigated frequently by the Ku Klux Klan and aimed at maintaining white supremacy by swift and terrible punishment of crimes of violence by Negroes against whites and especially against white women. But lynching, like opium, is habit-forming, and Southerners began to resort to lynching for relatively trivial offenses and to carry out those lynchings with the most revolting savagery and sadism.

This is a shameful blot on the South's record. But from 1900 on the number of lynchings went steadily down until in 1952 it reached zero.

The prediction that lynchings in the South would increase with the increasing tensions of the postwar era in the 1940's and 1950's did not materialize. The South quit the lynching habit because its people became more civilized and its sheriffs more efficient.

The other example of organized violence in the South is the Ku Klux Klan. There is no need here to go into its history or origin. There is about as much excuse for it nowadays as there would be for a low-grade moron with a machine gun at a church social.

Yet the Klan appears and disappears in accordance with the amount of racial tension existing at a particular time. Its trail in the South in the early 1950's was marked by cross-burnings, shootings, dynamitings and various forms of anti-

Catholic and anti-Negro violence, from Virginia to Florida.

At Myrtle Beach in Horry County, South Carolina, klansmen terrified Negroes and beat up a Negro night club operator. In the confusion a white police officer in klan regalia was shot and killed, whether by klansmen or others was never determined. Imperial Wizard Thomas L. Hamilton and half a dozen klansmen were indicted for inciting a riot, but the South Carolina jury refused to convict.

The Klan then instituted a reign of terror in Horry County, flogging both whites and Negroes for various reasons including "drinking too much" and "neglecting their families."

From northern South Carolina the Klan outrages spread to southern North Carolina. The pattern was the same. Gangs of cowardly and self-righteous thugs, under cover of darkness and hoods, took the law into their hands, invaded the homes and lashed the bodies of their fellow citizens, both white and colored, both men and women. Many cases of flogging were never reported, while others were reported tardily and reluctantly because the victims were afraid that those who had lashed them would come back and kill them if their crimes were reported to the authorities.

Many of these crimes were committed in Columbus County, North Carolina. Willard G. Cole, a newspaper editor in that county who kept up a courageous fight against the Klan when it was safer to keep quiet and inactive, wrote this about his experience:

"The twelve months from mid-January of 1951 to mid-January of 1952 were a continuous nightmare for me, for my wife and for many others in Columbus County. With me the fight that went on in that period was a fight of conviction rather than courage. What happens to one individual is not decisive, but what happens to American freedoms is tremendously significant. It couldn't happen to a fine people such as we have in Columbus, we thought. But it did. Masked men terrorized us; we lived behind locked doors and we kept weapons loaded. Just so this hooded terror might invade any community, unless hate, slander and prejudice are repulsed wherever and whenever they appear."

Southerners who had read with horror about what had happened in Hitler's Germany and Stalin's Russia woke up to the fact that it could happen, and was happening, in their own communities.

The State of North Carolina realized that the Klan's violence was directed not only against lowly and helpless individuals but also against the power and dignity of the State itself, and that for every blow which fell on the bared back of a Negro or a poor white, a still heavier blow fell on the back of the State. The State set to work in earnest to defend itself and its citizens. Solicitor Malcolm Seawell warned the Klansmen that if they broke into a person's home, or gained entry by deceit, in the nighttime for the purpose of flogging some victim, they would be tried for first-degree burglary, a capital offense.

In due course a number of Klansmen, together with the Imperial Wizard Hamilton were brought to trial before Judge Clawson Williams who said from the bench: "The time has not come in North Carolina when a man has to barricade himself in his home with the setting sun." Hamilton was sentenced to four years in prison and sixteen others given various sentences. The Klan in North Carolina had been, as some grand dragon might put it, "kaught, konquered, klobbered and dekapitated."

But the Klan will spring up again, in the South and elsewhere, whenever tension occurs and greedy men find it practical to organize fools in the service of intolerance and sadism. Like all organized crime, the Klan lives on public indifference and official apathy. It can always be crushed by

an alert public opinion which realizes that once the safe-
guards of the law are abrogated in favor of private notions,
passions and actions, no man is safe; and by public officials
who realize that the law must live up to what Richard
Hooker said of it long ago: "All things in heaven and earth
do her homage—the very least as feeling her care, the greatest
as not exempted from her power."

The South, especially in times of strained racial relations,
must guard against a recrudescence of lynching and the Klan,
as a member of Alcoholics Anonymous must guard against
liquor.

### Summary

What conclusions can be drawn regarding violence in the
South?

1. That the South is the most violent part of the United
States, leading other regions by a large margin in homicides
and aggravated assaults.

2. That the main cause of the South's pre-eminence is violence committed by Negroes against Negroes. Generally it
arises from trivial causes and is committed by the lower
class of Negroes. Both the Negroes themselves and the white
courts look on this situation with too much apathy.

3. The gathering of crime statistics should be improved.

4. An important contributing cause to Southern violence
is the easy availability of deadly weapons, especially shotguns
and knives.

5. The code of honor has practically nothing to do with
violence in the New South, the great bulk of the violence
being committed by people who are not interested in honor.

6. The South's Anglo-Saxon heritage contributes to its violence. Anglo-Saxons are naturally wild people who haven't
been tamed over here as they have been in England. The

frontier spirit lingers in the South and makes its contribution to the violence rate.

7. The Southern climate contributes to the high rate of crimes of violence, if only by bringing people together more than a colder climate would.

8. Patterns of violence, North and South, are distinct. In the North violence tends to be organized, in the South spontaneous. However, the South has engaged in two notorious kinds of organized violence—lynching and the Ku Klux Klan, both of which are at present quiescent but could flare up again in the absence of vigilance.

There is no excuse for the South's constant national leadership in violence. There is no excuse for Southerners maiming and murdering one another at the rate they do. There is no excuse for the indifference with which such crimes are regarded in the South. Both the South and its localities should take vigorous and far-reaching steps to correct this shameful condition. The South needs, first, to face the facts, and then to see what cure it can find in education, stricter law enforcement and other civilizing agencies.

# PART III

---

*WHAT IS THE SOUTH THINKING?*

# 11

## Race Dilemma:
## Equality vs. Excellence

A father had two sons in the Civil War, one fighting for the South, one for the North. Both died in battle. He buried them in one grave and placed above them this inscription: "Which was right, God only knows." Carl Sandburg told this story to Douglas S. Freeman, who said, "Both were right."

The main difficulty with the race problem in the South is that both sides are right.

The problem is essentially a conflict between two ideals— the ideal of excellence and the ideal of equality.

Two wrongs never make a right, but two rights, when they come in conflict, may make a terrible wrong.

Both whites and Negroes in the South are seeking a better way of life for themselves and their children. The end sought is the same, but the means are vastly different. The whites believe they can attain their aim through separation of the races in certain spheres, that is, by segregation. The Negroes believe they can attain their end by equality with the whites or by integration with them.

If the race problem in the South were a matter of bad men against good men, or prejudiced men against enlightened men, the South would be fortunate. The task of solving it would be comparatively simple. But it is not that at all.

Gunnar Myrdal toward the end of his *An American Dilemma* says: "When the author recalls the long gallery of persons whom, in the course for this inquiry, he has come to know with the impetuous but temporary intimacy of a stranger—sharecroppers and plantation owners, workers and employers, merchants and bankers, intellectuals, preachers, organization leaders, political bosses, gangsters, black and white, men and women, young and old, Southerners and Northerners—the general observation retained is the following: Behind all the outward dissimilarities, behind their contradictory valuations, rationalizations, vested interests, group allegiances and animosities, behind fears and defense constructions, behind the role they play in life and the mask they wear, the people are all much alike on a fundamental level. And they are all good people. They want to be rational and just. They plead to their consciences that they meant well even when things went wrong."

This is not a comforting thought. That Myrdal found that people on both sides of the race controversy were good men who wanted to be rational and just is as frightening as anything can be. It is precisely the sort of situation that sired the Civil War. When both sides are right, they can fight forever.

Indeed, the whole thing has all the earmarks of a Greek tragedy in which the hero or heroine is destroyed because he or she does precisely what is reasonable and right. Thus Antigone is destroyed for trying to bury the body of her brother, the traitor Polyneices, against the order of King Creon who condemned the body to lie in the street until it had been eaten by the dogs and vultures. An even better example is that of Prometheus, the Titan, who because he brought civilization to mankind, a lower order of beings, contrary to the decree of Zeus, is chained upon a mountain crag while birds of prey feed upon his vitals.

The Greek, Aeschylus, had a word for it when he said:

> With men or gods a mighty strife we strive
> Perforce, and either hap in grief concludes.

And again he said something nearly 2,500 years ago which sounds prophetic of the agitation of the race problem in the South today:                          •

> And strange is the Lord of Decision, who cleaveth the
>    birthright in twain—
> The edged thing, born of the North, the steel that is
>    ruthless and keen.

### What the Negro Wants

What does the Negro want? The answer is: everything. He wants everything the white man wants, including equal rights and privileges with him. He wants these things for himself, his wife and children, heirs, assigns and posterity. Nothing could be more natural or predictable.

Yet when this truth emerged from a book entitled *What the Negro Wants,* a symposium published by the University of North Carolina Press in 1944, it caused surprise and shock. There was, however, no doubt about the common want expressed. Writer after writer said the same thing. For example, Rayford W. Logan, the editor, concluded:

"In the name of democracy for all Americans we ask these irreducible fundamentals of first-class citizenship for all Negroes:

1. Equality of opportunity
2. Equal pay for equal work

3. Equal protection of the laws
4. Equality of suffrage
5. Equal recognition of the dignity of the human being
6. Abolition of public segregation

Leslie Pinckney Hill wrote: "What does the Negro want? Full citizen status in our American democracy."

George S. Schuyler, editor of the *Pittsburgh Courier,* observed: "As white supremacy seems to have become the religion of white America, so has social, political and economic equality become the religion of colored America."

A more strident, but probably quite as representative statement of the Negro's wants was made at the first meeting of the Niagara Movement in 1906:

"We shall not be satisfied with less than our full manhood rights . . . We want full manhood suffrage and we want it now. Second, we want discrimination in public accommodations to cease. Third, we claim the right of free men to associate with such people as wish to associate with us. Fourth, we want laws enforced against rich as well as poor, against capitalists as well as laborers, against white as well as black. We are not more lawless than the white race; we are more often arrested, convicted and mobbed. Fifth, we want our children educated. The school system of the country districts of the South is a disgrace to civilization, and in few towns and cities are the Negro schools what they ought to be."

The Negro then wants everything the white man wants, and the white man wants everything anybody wants.

## Issue is How to Attain Excellence

The issue in the race problem then is not one of wants since both races want the same things. The issue comes to this: The Southern whites believe they cannot maintain their present standards of civilization, except on the basis of segregation. These standards are often pitifully low, but they have been gradually lifted by the most strenuous exertions of a people plagued by problems of more than ordinary complexity, durability and contrariness.

The Southern whites and Negroes have been making slow but steady progress toward the good life since the bloody days of the Civil War and the darkness of the Reconstruction era, on the foundation of segregation. The whites emphatically do not want to try any experiments with that foundation, such as the mixing of the races in public schools, and they will go to considerable lengths to prevent any tampering with that foundation by outside forces.

The present Negro leadership, at least in the North, on the contrary apparently believes that the progress of their race toward the good life depends on putting an end to public segregation without delay. This would seem to be the logical explanation of the argument that equal but separate facilities in school and elsewhere for whites and Negroes would still be discrimination against Negroes. Such an argument may be rational, and may indeed be correct, but it sounds suspiciously as if the Negro leadership by espousing it has adopted the theory of white supremacy; otherwise, if the Negro is the equal of the white man why should he not make equal progress toward the good life, given equal facilities? A corollary question arises: If the Negro is entitled to lift himself by enforced association with the white man, why should not the white man be entitled to prevent himself from being pulled down by enforced association with the Negro?

Incidentally, it might be observed that intimate proximity of the races tends to make the good persons of both races better and the bad ones worse.

## Burden of Proof is on Segregation

The burden of proof is on the South to show that segregation is necessary in each of the fields in which it is practiced. Segregation should not be enforced without evidence of necessity, and its pains should be mitigated whenever and wherever practicable. For the truth is that segregation is cruel and costly. The American genius and the Christian spirit tend alike to take men as they are without distinction of race, creed or fortuitous differences.

St. Peter, after his vision of the variety of creatures let down to earth in a sheet, said, "But God hath showed me that I should not call any man common or unclean."

It is not pleasant for a man—at least, one of good will—to say to another, "You are my inferior and so must be limited by law and custom in your association with me," nor may the opinion of inferiority be tenable because, in the first place, men are compounded of many qualities and one is likely to be superior to another in some of them and inferior in others, and because, in the second place, few, if any, are impartial judges in such a matter. This applies also to races. The white South is not comfortable in insisting on segregation in the face of a world-wide demand for equality. It would be much easier for it to say, with Mark Twain, "I have no prejudices—no class prejudice, no religious prejudice, no race prejudice. All I want to know about a man is that he is a human being, he couldn't be worse."

## The Southern Dilemma

Nevertheless, the South must ask itself very earnestly whether it can afford to do away with segregation in certain fields, especially public education. Other parts of the country, such as New England, where the Negro is an inconsiderable part of the population, may accept social equality without qualms as a theory and without much disruption as a practical matter. But the South, at least those parts with a heavy proportion of Negroes, is "confronted with a condition, not a theory."

The South is right in the middle of this genuine and painful dilemma: If the South insists on retaining segregation, it must look forward to a long and costly fight with the N.A.A.C.P., perhaps the Federal Government, and indirectly with world opinion; on the other hand, if the South should accept integration of the races, it might wake up to find that its progress toward the good life for itself and its posterity had been set back indefinitely or destroyed. The South cannot evade this dilemma, and it cannot afford to be mistaken in its choice.

Another phase of the dilemma is political. It poses an acute problem in those parts of the South where Negroes are more than 50 per cent of the population, sometimes a great deal more. The Southern white man subscribes in theory to the principle that all men are equal before the law, but he balks at extending that principle to the ballot box when such extension might foreseeably result in turning over his local government to a race which has little education and no experience in government. He is apprehensive of what such a government might do to his person, his family, his home and his property.

The South does not hope for much sympathy or help in this fearful dilemma in which, to quote Thomas Jefferson, "justice is in the one scale and self-preservation in the other," but she does ask for the sort of appreciation of the problem by other parts of the country that Lincoln showed in 1854 when he said of the Negro and slavery: "If all earthly power were given me I should not know what to do as to the existing situation."

## The Exact Issue

What exactly is the race problem in the South? Would it help to define it more strictly? Let us try to get at what it is by seeing what it is not.

First, it is not a problem of individuals, although it touches them deeply. Southern whites would admit that there are vast differences in individuals and that certain Negroes are superior to certain whites. Yet the individual by law and custom is classified, not according to his qualifications, but according to his race.

Second, the problem is not one of color precisely, although color is its sign and symbol. That is, the South does not contend that a race approaches perfection in direct ratio to its blondness, or imperfection in proportion to the darkness of its epidermis. The South, probably more than other parts of the country, practices social equality with Jews, Chinese and Hindus, who are darker than the Anglo-Saxon strain predominant in the South. It is interesting to speculate what would have happened if the Negro population in the South had from the beginning been Chinese or Jewish. It may be suspected that by now the level of the intellectual, commercial and cultural life of the South would be far higher than it is, and that, if the races had separate schools, the Anglo-Saxons would be clamoring to get in the Jewish or Chinese schools rather than vice versa.

Third, the problem is not quite the biological one it is often cracked up to be. A good deal of satire has been poked at the supposed belief of Southern whites that if segregation were banished in favor of social equality on some certain day, this would be a signal for white women and Negro men or white men and Negro women to rush into one another's arms, with a new mulatto population springing from the miscegenation. A few whites, it is true, talk as if they fear something of the sort, and practically all of them are determined to prevent the mingling of white girls and women with Negro boys and men on a social basis. However, the prime motive of the South in insisting on retaining segregation is probably not so much a fear of mass miscegenation as it is a fear that white standards, in various fields ranging from schools to government, would deteriorate most dangerously as the result of the influx of overwhelming numbers of Negroes accustomed to lower standards.

So much for what the problem is not. But what is it? Essentially it is the problem of the coexistence of two races, or rather peoples, in close proximity—one of them a mixture of peoples (mainly Anglo-Saxon and Western European) whose history shows very great achievements in science, philosophy, economics, government, literature and art, and the other a comparatively primitive people. The white South balks at exchanging its European-American culture for an African brand, or of diluting it too much.

Three theories concerning the Negro's condition in America are widely held, as Wm. T. Couch points out in his publisher's introduction to *What The Negro Wants*. They are:

1. The Negro's condition is caused by his inherent inferiority, which cannot be overcome.

2. This inferiority can be overcome, and the prejudice, which results from it, can be cured.

3. The Negro is not inferior, but only appears so because of the disabilities inflicted on him by the white man; his condition is solely a result of race prejudice.

Most sociologists and anthropologists hold the third view, but most white Southerners probably hold the first and some hold the second. "Which is right, God only knows."

## Negro's Virtues and Vices

There is in the South a diversity of peoples. As one individual differs from another, so one race differs greatly from another, some sociologists and anthropologists to the contrary notwithstanding.

The Negroes in the South have certain virtues (together with the vices which, according to Aristotle's insight, are those virtues' excesses.)

For instance:

1. Patience. A Negro named Ben Long, for whom I once acted as attorney, had been hit in the head with a sledge hammer by a fellow worker while he was repairing a railroad track. He was sitting by the fire in his cabin when I went to see him to prepare his case; he was completely paralyzed and likely to stay that way the rest of his life. A white man would have been cursing his luck. But Ben was mainly impressed by the fact that he was still alive. He kept saying, "Tain't nothing but the mercy of God!" Such patience, springing from resignation to fate, has a survival value. Other races may disappear but Ben's will probably be able to say tens of thousands of years hence, "We endured."

But the vice of patience is lack of initiative, and if the Southern Negro has more than his share of endurance, he has less than his share of initiative.

2. Kindness. It is the sort of kindness that goes out to those in need, and another name for it is charity. The Negro in the South often looks out for those members of his family, and indeed his race, who by reason of sickness, hard luck or any other kind of adversity are down and out. It is a spontaneous, personal thing, not a calculated, and certainly not an institutionalized, matter. It extends especially to the old and to children. Many Negro families are housing, clothing

and feeding other Negroes who have little or no claim on them except the claim of common humanity.

Yet the reverse of this virtue is the encouragement of improvidence, laziness and immorality—old people without savings and children without fathers. Nevertheless, the charity is there and it rarely fails altogether.

3. Joyfulness. Negroes get more fun out of the simple joys of life than white people do—doubtless they have to in order to stand it at all. Joyfulness is a sort of virtue; at any rate the joyful person is frequently close to the source of life.

But in the Negro this joyfulness is part of an emotionalism which, when it turns sour, makes for irresponsibility and unconsidered violence. Thus the Negro will cut up his friend and then make his plea in court that he only "stroked him with a razor." Many woundings, maimings and killings arise from the most trivial causes, or no cause. "What was the trouble between you?" the prosecuting attorney asks the defendant who did the cutting, and the prosecuting witness, who is swathed in bandages from the waist up. The standard answer from both parties is, "No trouble at all." Quite often it is true. They were, and are, the best of friends.

These traits are not necessarily racial, but they are traits of Southern Negroes as conditioned by the Southern biracial culture. Nor do these traits manifest themselves in all Southern Negroes. Still, they are recognizable traits.

### The Argument for Segregation

The argument of the whites for segregation may be based on something besides prejudice. To understand the problem one must understand the reasoning back of the Southern white man's position. Perhaps the following may give some idea of how they arrive at their position:

What is segregation? Something that happens, more or

less, in all societies, according to custom and regardless of laws. It can always be mitigated—and should be—but it is not likely to be altogether eliminated.

What is equality? A fiction, except in mathematics. As applied to persons it does not exist. No person is equal to any other person in body, mind or spirit, as a wise and merciful Providence has decreed. The essence of an individual is his inequality. An individual is an individual.

Why then talk about "all men are created equal"? Because, while the concept is a legal fiction, it is an indispensable one. It is the foundation stone of our system of constitutional democracy. All men are equal in the sight of the law; all are endowed by their Creator with certain rights—few but elementary—which no government can take away from them, nor can their possessors bargain them away; that is what Jefferson meant.

But is this "equality" a means or an end? Evidently not an end. Nobody would work toward an equality on the bottom, a leveling down. But if it is a means, what is it for? It is a means for self-defense and for opportunity; therefore it is a means to freedom.

But is freedom a means or an end? Evidently not an end. One does not want to be free for nothing, but for something. For what? For making the best of himself, for realizing his latent possibilities up to the bounds of his inherent limitations. The end, in a word, is excellence.

This brings us back to the crucial point. The Negroes may look on "equality" with the whites as a means to excellence, but the whites do not look on equality with the Negroes as a means to excellence for themselves.

Thus a great many white people in the South strongly believe that the quality of education would suffer severely if the races were mixed in the public schools. This belief is an honest one and is not motivated by hate. On the contrary, many who hold it are sincerely friendly to the Negro and want to help his progress rather than to impede it.

But they see the main objective of the public schools as excellence, not equality, and they look on discrimination and segregation as inherent qualities of education, regardless of race. Thus every examination and promotion tends to separate the bright child from the dull in order to give each pupil a better chance to bring out whatever excellence he may have in him.

The viewpoint of the Southern whites is based partly on experience, partly on history. They do not deny that there are individuals among the Negroes who are far above the average of the whites in intellect and ability. But they do not think the average of the two races is the same.

They note that in the course of history Greece produced Plato, Pericles and Aristotle; Italy produced Caesar, Dante and Aquinas; France produced Abelard, Montaigne and Joan of Arc; Germany produced Bach, Beethoven and Goethe; England produced Shakespeare, Newton and Churchill; America produced Jefferson, Lincoln and Lee; Poland produced Copernicus, Conrad and Marie Curie; Russia produced Tolstoy, Chekov and Dostoyevsky; India produced Gautama Buddha, the anonymous author of the Katha Upanishad, and Gandhi; China produced Li Tai Po, Confucius and Lao Tze; the Jews produced Moses, Paul, Spinoza, Kant and Einstein.

But then many people ask: What have the Negro people, in Africa, produced to compare with what these other peoples have produced in their own countries? And they have no satisfactory answer.

Southerners doubtless would admit that the Creator of mankind could whenever He pleased make a race or a people shine in the firmament of history as brilliantly as a nova shines in the night sky, and that He could raise the Negroes to greatness as He did the Greeks and the Normans, but until there are more signs that this is coming to pass the whites in the South are inclined to seek excellence through segregation rather than through amalgamation.

### *Approaches to the Problem*

What can be done about the problem? Many approaches to a solution have been suggested. Here are some of them:

1. Diffusion. R. Beverly Herbert of Columbia, South Carolina says in *What We Can Do About The Race Problem:* "Since race fear is at the root of race hatred and this fear is the greatest where Negro populations are heaviest, the migration of Negroes from sections having the largest proportionate populations to sections where the Negro percentage is small, should be encouraged. This could be done by federal appropriations providing transportation and for subsidence in new localities."

This is, of course, being done now "by federal appropriations," although not in the way Mr. Herbert envisions. War industries, which are dependent on federal money, are drawing large masses of Negroes from the South to Northern cities, such as New York, Chicago, Cleveland, Pittsburgh and Detroit. Probably the diffusion of Negroes through migration will do more to solve, or at least ameliorate, the insolvable problem than anything else can.

2. Mitigation of segregation in certain fields. As a matter of fact, there is much more segregation now than there used to be, not because anyone planned it that way, but because inflation and labor-saving devices make for much less domestic service by Negroes in the homes of whites and also because urban life is far more compartmentalized than it used to be, or than country life and small town life are. Whites and Negroes are not thrown together as much as they

used to be. There are various fields, including transportation, in which the callous and senseless effects of segregation could, and should, be mitigated.

Dr. Howard W. Odum suggests that an inquiry be made to explore and catalogue "the extreme range of illogical and inexcusable injustices . . . the hazards and difficulties involved . . . the limitations and deficiencies of the Negro as well as his superiorities . . . the interregional ramifications . . . and the costs of conversion."

3. Better enforcement of the Negro's legal rights. This includes his right to vote, when properly qualified, his right to freedom from intimidation by violence, his right to sit on juries, and so on.

4. Equalization of educational facilities. The courts furnish the Southern states strong motives for this.

5. Extension of the progress the Negro has made in the economic life of the South. He has made much progress in agriculture and stands ready to make much more in the near future. In commerce and the professions he has been doing fairly well; Negro businesses have multiplied and so have Negro doctors, lawyers, dentists, journalists, et cetera, but the near future holds the promise of far more progress along this line.

In industry, however, the record is spotty. In some industries the Negro is much in demand, notably the steel, lumber and tobacco industries; in others, such as the textile business which employs large numbers of women, he has been generally excluded. Yet as industry seeks less industrialized areas for its new plants, as in eastern North Carolina, Alabama and Mississippi, and as the industrialization of the nation increases faster than the labor supply does, it may well be that the Negro will be more in demand as a laborer than he has been in certain industries, and that by force of circumstances, if for no other reason, he will get a fairer chance in industry than he has had in the past.

6. The Negro should place the emphasis on true, not fictional, equality. Davis Lee, a Negro, publisher of the Newark, New Jersey *Telegram,* makes this argument:

"The entire race problem in America is wrong. Our approach is wrong. We expend all our energies and spend millions of dollars trying to convince white people that we are as good as they are, that we are an equal. Joe Louis is not looked upon as a Negro, but as the greatest fighter of all times, loved and admired by whites in South Carolina as much as by those in Michigan. He convinced the world, not by propaganda, but by demonstration.

"Our fight for recognition, justice, civil rights and equality should be carried on within the race. Let us demonstrate to the world by our living standards, our conduct, our ability and intelligence that we are the equal of any man, and when we shall have done this the entire world, including the South, will accept us on our terms. Our present program of threats and agitation makes enemies of our friends."

There is a good deal of truth in this. "Social equality" is a phrase, and a very hazy one at that. Aesop's dog crossing a bridge over a stream saw his reflection in the water with the bone in its mouth, and while opening his jaws to seize the reflection lost the reality. The Negro in the South may well ask himself whether he is in danger of losing the tangible gains he has made if he loosens his grasp on them in order to reach for something called "social equality." After all, excellence is better than equality. Excellence is the end, while equality is only one possible means. It is not sensible to redouble one's means while forgetting one's aim.

7. Outside interference may sometimes do more harm than good. The problem is difficult enough without being complicated by those who "darken counsel with words without

knowledge." The less outside interference there is, the more the work of the moderates in the South, both colored and white, will be facilitated. The more outside interference of the uninformed or fire-eating sort there is, the greater will be the power of the Southern extremists and race baiters.

Dr. H. W. Odum believes that the South, "moving surely toward the guarantee of equal opportunity, in the face of bitter attack and vested frustration by many irresponsibles isolated from the realities of living democracy," will succeed in protecting "the great mass of Negroes from outsiders who would weaken or destroy their extraordinary system of schools, churches, industry and self-developed programs which have amazed the world by their mastery and by the effectiveness of their training grounds for progress and leadership."

And Editor Davis Lee says, "At present the white man is definitely in the Negro's corner, and he not only wants to see him get ahead, he is helping him. But continued agitation and unwarranted pressure will turn him against the Negro."

8. Tolerance, patience and good will. Only through an approach using these qualities on both sides does the problem offer any hope of being solved at all. Chancellor Edward K. Graham of the Woman's College of the University of North Carolina rightly said, "the more serious the issue, the greater the necessity for keeping our emotional balance, our good humor and our perspective." It will not be easy.

It will help if people outside the South will assume that white Southerners are no less "liberal, generous and decent" than they themselves are, and realize, to quote Mr. Herbert again, that "we have a great sociological problem to deal with and not a mere petty prejudice; a problem that has done infinite harm and that will require our greatest qualities to solve."

The Civil War is a terrible example of what happens when both sides are right.

The North was right because the Union had to be preserved; the South was right because the North had no constitutional power to stop her from seceding and destroying the Union.

The North was right because slavery was a vicious anachronism which had to be abolished; the South was right because the North had no constitutional authority to abolish slavery, and because it offered the South no alternative to slavery except social and economic chaos.

Each side was convinced of its rectitude; therefore the war was a long and bloody one.

It could have been averted only if the moderates, in both the North and the South, had kept control. But once the secessionists in the South and the abolitionists in the North became stronger than the moderates, all hope of peace was lost.

The race problem in the South is another example of the danger inherent in a conflict when both sides are right. The Negroes may be right in thinking they can make faster progress by abolishing segregation, the whites in believing they can make faster progress by retaining it.

The best hope of an accommodation, if not a solution, lies in the moderates; the grave danger lies in the trend of power away from the moderates and toward the extremists on both sides.

# 12

## From Monticello to Bilbo

We hold these truths to be self-evident.—Thomas Jefferson, 1776.

Let us raise a standard to which the wise and honest can repair.—George Washington, 1787.

[My opponent is] a cross between a hyena and a mongrel . . . begotten in a nigger graveyard at midnight, suckled by a sow, and educated by a fool.—Theodore G. Bilbo, Mississippi, 1934.

Frequently strike a pose with arms outstretched, fists clenched, head thrown back, and eyes turned toward heaven. This position carries the subtle suggestion of receiving inspiration from above. It suggests, ever so delicately, that the speaker is merely the medium through which a message from on high is being transmitted to the audience below.—Governor Fuller Warren of Florida: *How To Win In Politics,* 1949.

Something happened to Southern politics and politicians between 1776 and 1950. It was not funny but it reminds one of the story of the railroad worker testifying in a case of the death of a fellow workman who had been run over by a train. "I walked down the track," he said, "and came across one of Jim's arms. Then I went on and came across one of Jim's legs and a little later I came across his head." "What did you think then?" the lawyer asked. "Well, I thought to myself," he said, "something serious has happened to Jim."

Something serious happened to Southern statecraft.

Between 1776 and 1850 the South gave the nation (and in a sense, the world) a brand of statesmanship which is not easily matched in any period of history, anywhere. The men who were the chief architects of the American Government, an imposing number of the men who designed the great edifice and provided it with a continent for its foundation—Peyton Randolph, Patrick Henry, George Washington, Thomas Jefferson, James Madison, John Marshall, Andrew Jackson and James K. Polk—were Southerners.

But from 1850 the South became engrossed in defending its "peculiar institution," slavery. It ceased thinking nationally and began thinking sectionally; it ceased thinking creatively and started thinking defensively; it stopped thinking with its head and started thinking with its nerves. Its actions became reflex actions. Every time the North whispered, "Abolition," the South rushed out of its mansion waving a saber. Such a life was not conducive to the contemplation essential to consistent statesmanship.

Not long before the Civil War the South lost its ability to think in terms of national politics, an ability it had demonstrated so brilliantly for three-fourths of a century. If it had retained it, there would have been no Civil War—perhaps a revolt in the deep South and some skirmishes but nothing very serious or durable. However, the epigoni replaced the elite, and the war was on.

The South, having lost its ability to think, then proceeded to lose everything else. "Whom the gods would destroy, they first make mad."

How can Southern politics in the past century, fantastic and incredible as it has been, be explained?

### South Changed Its Form of Government

As a result of its defeat in the Civil War the South changed not only its form of government but also its philosophy of government. This is something which has not happened elsewhere in the United States before or since. It was not a change of personalities or administrations. There was nothing superficial about it. It went to the roots of political life. It was a destruction of the old political edifice "from turret to foundation stone," and later the construction of an entirely new building, with the foundation stones becoming the turrets and the turrets the mudsills.

In other words, it was a change from an aristocratic to a democratic form of government.

Mobocracy was the intermediate stage between aristocracy and democracy. The South felt mobocracy in its full force and ferocity.

The vote which was taken away from the most responsible Southern whites was transferred to their former slaves. It was a spectacle, as a Northern newspaper said, of "barbarism overwhelming civilization by physical force." A combination of Northern idealists and opportunists, leagued with ignorant and relatively innocent Negroes, provided for the South the sort of government that is not seen except in upheavals such as have occurred after revolutions, and rarely then.

That is why the South understands probably better than other parts of the nation today the dangers of defeat in war and the plight of various European countries.

"The Southerners," said the editor of *Scribner's Monthly,* after a trip through the South during the Reconstruction Era, "feel that they were wronged, that they have no future.

that they cannot protect themselves and that nothing but death or voluntary exile awaits them."

Carl Schurz saw in the South "a usurpation such as this country has never seen, and probably no citizen of the United States has ever seen, and probably no citizen of the United States has ever dreamed of."

Reference to the terrible and tragic Reconstruction Era is made here, not to fight the Civil War over again or to parade the woes of the South, but to explain Southern politics, even today.

The South did not like that part of the Democratic platform of 1952 which said: "However, we believe that the Federal Government should take supplemental action within constitutional jurisdiction to oppose discrimination against race, religion or national origin."

Well, why not? Why should the South object to civil rights including a compulsory fair employment practices act? Why should it object to them so strongly that several Southern states deserted the Democratic party, their Ark of the Covenant, in 1948 to become Dixiecratic, and others did so in 1952? It looks almost pathological.

The answer of course lies in history. The South's fears of civil rights legislation go back to the Reconstruction days. Not all Southerners have forgotten the Civil Rights Act, concocted by Sumner and signed by Grant on March 1, 1875, providing for mixed schools and equal rights for Negroes in hotels, theaters, public conveyances and public conveniences. The Federal Government was preparing to enforce it by armed might until the United States Supreme Court held it unconstitutional.

The South is forgetting but it has not quite forgotten. History is easily forgotten by those who have not had it jump on them. But those who have felt its heels in their back remember it for quite a while.

This Reconstruction orgy of greed and graft was of course too absurd and terrible to last. It was overthrown by a counteroffensive of Southern whites led by the old aristocrats, using such fantastic organizations as the Ku Klux Klan, the Red Shirts and the Knights of the White Camelia. But the aristocratic class could not keep an aristocratic form of government going. They failed for the same reasons the same class in various European countries failed to do the same thing after the First and Second World Wars. The Southern aristocrats had lost the war and with it their prestige and their wealth which was a very important source of their power. Furthermore, they had little to offer the people; the people wanted schools, roads, jobs, health and so on, while the upper class was more interested in conservation than development.

There were many very good men in this aristocratic class in the South, but they were not cut out for the task before them. David MacRae, in *The Americans at Home,* written a few years after the Civil War, said: "A stranger passing from the North meets, on the one hand, a lordlier class of men than the North has been able to produce—lordlier perhaps than the South, devoid now of a servile class over which to rear its head, can ever in this age produce again—a class as nearly approaching our own nobility as was possible in the midst of cotton-growing and slavery." And Emerson, speaking of this class in the South, said: "Men who were too great to be bullied or bribed gave way to lordliness. This was the power of the South. The North was talked down by these agreeable gentlemen. War was the disinfectant to this serious infection."

### Dance of the Demagogues

The disinfectant wiped out the infection but left worse germs behind.

A yapping pack of Southern demagogues arose from the ruins of the aristocracy. Their names were legion, but a few gaudy samples are "Pitchfork Ben" Tillman, "The Man" Bilbo, "Cotton Ed" Smith, and "Gene" Talmadge.

Billingsgate was their meat and soft soap their dessert. The black man was their shield and buckler, an ever present help in time of trouble. With neither character nor ability to recommend them, they could usually win in a tight election by raising the cry of "nigger" and scaring the masses of voters by insinuating that if the other fellow was elected, they would find their children sitting beside "niggers" in grade school. They had "a class appeal without a class program."

"Pitchfork Ben" Tillman, who dominated South Carolina politics for thirty years, during which time he was Governor of South Carolina and the Palmetto State's Nessus-shirt gift to the United States Senate, got his name and his start by promising that if the voters would send him to Washington he would "stick his pitchfork" in the ribs of Grover Cleveland, President of the United States.

Tillman's brother shot and killed N. G. Gonzales, editor of *The State* (Columbia, South Carolina) because he could not longer stand Gonzales' taunts about the way he and his brother were debauching the government of his state. The people of South Carolina responded by clearing the murderer before a jury and erecting a monument to the victim. Thus the populace was satisfied.

Theodore "The Man" Bilbo of Mississippi served as State Senator, Lieutenant Governor, Governor and U. S. Senator. He was also a licensed but unordained Baptist preacher. He was also an unabashed crook, with probably the most vitriolic tongue in the country. During his first term as Governor there was gossip about his prowess with women. Far from denying it or keeping silent, Bilbo made a speech to an audience of women in which he said, "If these stories about the man Bilbo are true, you've got to admit, sisters, that he's a man." After that he began calling himself "The Man."

Charged with racial and religious prejudice, Bilbo was reported in a dispatch from Leland, Mississippi, as saying he was "for every damn Jew from Jesus Christ on down."

In the LeRoy Percy-James K. Vardaman campaign for the United States Senate in 1910, Bilbo boasted that he accepted a bribe to vote for Percy but had not kept the bargain. It was later proved that some of the bills were issued after the day on which Bilbo said he had accepted them. The Mississippi legislature pronounced him "unfit to sit with honest, upright men in a respectable legislative body" and requested him to resign. He did not resign; all this merely furthered his political career.

How can one explain that? William Alexander Percy, son of LeRoy Percy, explained it as follows in *Lanterns on the Levee:*

"The man responsible for tearing father's reputation to tatters and saddening three lives was a pert little monster, glib and shameless, with that sort of cunning common to criminals which passes for intelligence. The people loved him. They loved him not because they were deceived in him, but because they understood him thoroughly; they said of him proudly, 'He's a slick little bastard.' He was one of them . . ."

The Southern demagogue is a phenomenon of a region in process of changing its form of government. It takes quite a while. Bilbo is an extreme example but most of them are extreme, fantastic and incredible in a society which is supposed to be civilized and a democracy.

The South was short on bread and circuses. The dema-

gogues weren't interested in providing the bread but they
were wonderful at putting on the circuses. Virulence and
vulgarity were their stock in trade. "Our Bob" Reynolds of
North Carolina kissed Jean Harlow for the benefit of pho-
tographers on the Capitol steps in Washington. Governor
"Kissin' Jim" Folsom kissed everybody in sight in Alabama.
Reynolds beat Governor Cameron Morrison of North Carolina for the United States Senate by campaigning in a battered, antique Ford, accusing his wealthy opponent of eating
caviar ("you know, that's fish eggs") and mocking him in his
speeches by making a lordly gesture of rolling out an imaginary red carpet from the Morrison limousine to the Morrison mansion.

The old Kentuckian who said, "Tom Jefferson is forgot;
Calhoun and Clay are dead—and I ain't feelin' so well myself!" expressed the feeling of a good many Southerners.

### How Did the Demagogues Do It?

If diplomacy is "the art of the possible," Southern politics
must have been the art of the incredible as practiced by the
unspeakable. How did these creatures keep their power?

It is easy to see how they got that power. They got it by
revolution imposed from outside the region; revolution pre-
sents unrivaled opportunity for their type. They got it by
vituperation of better men and they got it by promises. But
since they kept no promises, how did they keep the voters?

Various explanations occur:

1. The ignorance of the voters. According to *Scribner's
Statistical Atlas of the United States* (New York, 1883), the
percentages of the population in the Southern states in 1880
above ten years of age who were unable to read or write were
as follows:

| State | White | Colored |
|---|---|---|
| Virginia | 18 | 74 |
| North Carolina | 32 | 77 |
| South Carolina | 22 | 78 |
| Georgia | 23 | 82 |
| Florida | 21 | 71 |
| Alabama | 25 | 81 |
| Mississippi | 17 | 75 |
| Louisiana | 20 | 79 |
| Texas | 14 | 75 |
| Arkansas | 25 | 75 |
| Tennessee | 28 | 72 |

A region with a sizable proportion of ignorant and illiterate people is the demagogue's happy hunting ground. It is not fruitful soil for democracy.

2. Race prejudice. The demagogues exploited the race issue to a fare-you-well. When everything else failed, the demagogue could win by playing on the racial fears of the poor and insecure whites—the fear of social equality and the fear of racial amalgamation.

3. Class prejudice. The poor whites who were forbidden to enter the colonel's front door were naturally ripe for picking by the colonel's opponent in an election. All pretense to honor and decency was thrown out of the window. The demagogue got down not only to the people's level but below it. "My opponent," said one at a political meeting, "has charged that I will not tell you people where I stand on any issue. That's a lie. I will tell you right now where I stand on every issue. If a thing is right, I am for it." (Here he waited for applause, but none was forthcoming.) "If a thing is wrong, I am against it." (Again he waited for applause from his audience—in vain.) "And if that platform doesn't suit you, ladies and gentlemen, just let me know and I will be glad to change it."

4. Promises. It was easy enough to promise the people all the things they wanted—the necessities of life were about all they asked for. But it was not easy to fulfill those promises. Therefore, the rabble-rousers who identified themselves with the poor and promised them land, schools, roads, jobs, high prices for their crops, freedom from debt, taxes and so on, found it easier and more profitable to sell out to the "interests" than to help their people. So they did sell out and became conservative, counting on short memories to keep the gullible grappled to their side.

There was one of them, Huey Long, who fulfilled some of his promises to the people, though at a high cost of liberty and honesty in government. "He kept faith with the people," according to V. O. Key, author of *Southern Politics,* "and they with him. He gave them something and the corporations paid for it."

What Huey Long told his people under the Evangeline Oak back in 1928 had the ring of sincerity to it:

"Where are the schools that you have waited for your children to have, that have never come? Where are the roads and highways that you spent your money to build, that are no nearer now than ever before? Where are the institutions to care for the sick and disabled? Evangeline wept bitter tears in her disappointment, but it lasted through only one lifetime. Your tears in this country, around this oak, have lasted for generations. Give me the chance to dry the eyes of those who still weep here!"

That is why the people of Louisiana gave their votes to Huey Long in "preference to better men who neglected them altogether."

In the end, however, Huey came high. He and his gang seized "unprecedented power" in a state of the United States and used it for purposes of unprecedented corruption. Huey predicted toward the close of his career that his associates would go to the penitentiary "if he were not there to hold them down," and quite a lot of them did.

### Rocky Road to Democracy

Most of the South after the Civil War went from aristocracy to riff-raffistocracy without touching democracy on the way.

Not all of it did, however. Virginia has pretty well stuck to the aristocratic-oligarchic form of government through thick and thin, up to date. "A Political Museum Piece" is what Key calls Virginia's government in his *Southern Politics*. He admits it has its virtues:

"The oligarchy that rules Virginia demonstrates a sense of honor, an aversion to open venality, a degree of sensitivity to public opinion, a concern for efficiency in administration and, so long as it does not cost much, a feeling of social responsibility."

This system also has its defects. "A smaller proportion of that state's electorate votes for governor than does that of any other state in the South," which is saying *multum in parvo*. The big stick of the Byrd machine is its patronage power and its power to set salaries, within minimum-maximum brackets established by law, of hundreds of county officials. Thus as the chauffeurs of the machine admit, the local politicians are kept "in an understanding and sympathetic frame of mind."

In brief, the Virginia system has provided the Old Dominion with honest and fairly efficient government—no mean accomplishment in our day and time—but it has run roughshod over good men who have got in its path, and it has, with its emphasis on governmental economy amounting to penuriousness, failed to provide the people with the services they needed.

North Carolina is another exception to the general rule in

the South. It made the transition from aristocracy to democracy fairly quickly and easily because it did not have far to move.

Much of this was due to a widespread conviction that government should be responsive to the needs of all the people and that education and industry must make progress together. The symbol of this belief, and indeed its voice, was Charles B. Aycock, who was Governor of North Carolina from 1901 to 1905.

He set the progressive tone for North Carolina state government in the first year of the present century, and by and large the State has stayed on key. Since his administration, Tar Heel Governors have been on the progressive bandwagon; some have held the reins a little tightly while others have whipped the horses, but none has tried to put on the brakes or spike the wheels. "A Progressive Plutocracy" is the designation given North Carolina by V. O. Key in *Southern Politics,* and it probably is one, but the accent since Aycock has always been on the "progressive." Aycock was a "corporation lawyer" as various other North Carolina Governors —Morrison, Gardner, Ehringhaus, Hoey, Broughton, Cherry and Umstead—were after him, but the fact that North Carolina has high corporation taxes, the proceeds of which go to various state services for all the people, is indication that these Governors put their state above their clients.

The result has been that the people felt no need to call on would-be dictators or mountebanks to help them throw off an oppressive upper class. It was not necessary that a candidate be a hypocrite or a demagogue to be elected to high office in North Carolina, whereas in quite a few other Southern states the worst candidates consistently won.

In South Carolina, Georgia, Alabama, Louisiana and Mississippi, for instance, the "wool-hat boys" had a habit of electing one of their own crowd who later would turn out to

be just another tool of the silk-hat bosses. Such was the rule
to which North Carolina and Virginia provided the exceptions.

In the past two decades the South has made much political
progress in that it has learned to do two things. It has
learned to operate the strange machine called democracy, at
home, and it has learned to think nationally and internation-
ally at Washington.

Southerners in Congress no longer look on themselves as
ambassadors from their sovereign states to a foreign (and
semihostile) nation. On the contrary, during the interna-
tional upheavals since about 1935, they have done a good job
of thinking and voting on foreign affairs. It was fortunate
for the nation and Western Civilization that they did.

If evidence of this is needed, it may be found in the editorial comment of a New York newspaper:

"The recent record of the South in world affairs is inspiring. Lend-lease would have been beaten in Congress without
Southern votes. When the first year of the first draft expired,
four months before Pearl Harbor, it was Southern members
of Congress that insured its extension. When by one vote
Congress decided not to send the soldiers home, it was the
South that turned the scale. Representatives of twelve Southern states cast 102 votes in favor of extending the draft and
only six votes against it."

The South is sending better men to Washington now than
it has been accustomed to send at any time since 1860. That
is not a difficult task, because for the better part of a century
the South seemed hell-bent on sending, in retaliation, the
sort of men to represent it in the nation's capital that the
North sent the South in the Reconstruction Era. This helps
explain the Bilbos, Longs, McKellars, Rankins *et al.* The
improvement can be seen by contrasting the new type of
Southerners in Congress—e.g., Hill, Sparkman, Kefauver,

Russell, Fulbright—with the old type. The South no longer feels that it has to avenge itself by sending insults to Washington in the form of Senators and Representatives.

Strangely enough, the Midwest seems to be taking over the role which the South is abandoning; the Midwest irresponsibles of the McCarthy-Jenner type are quite reminiscent of the vanishing irresponsibles of the South.

But let us not rose-tint the Southern picture. The South does not yet send its really best men to Washington; it rather tends to keep them at home and export its militant mediocrities. When it sends a really first-rate man, by accident—as North Carolina did with the appointment of Frank P. Graham to the United States Senate—it is so shocked by this breach of an old Southern custom that it immediately takes him back again.

But the South is learning, slowly and painfully, to work the strange machinery of the democratic form of government.

# 13

## Main Currents in Southern
## Thought—1850–1953

What of the Southern mind? How does it
work? What do Southerners think about? What of the quality of their thinking? Is the Southern mind a Sargasso Sea,
or are there strong currents moving in it?

In general Southern thought has been more concrete than
abstract, more pragmatic than speculative, more conservative than adventurous, more traditional than radical. It has
been concerned more with pressing problems than with pure
thought, more interested in government, economics, a code
of conduct and a way of life than in philosophy, science, religion or art. In many ways, strange to say, it has been more
realistic than idealistic, more practical than sentimental.
Transcendentalism was a Northern, not a Southern, phenomenon.

I think these generalizations are valid, even if, as Adrienne
Koch contends, the "philosopher-statesmen" Jefferson and
Madison made the greatest contribution that has ever been
made to American philosophy, the theme of which is "ex-

perimental humanism." If they were profound thinkers they
were also very practical ones.

Throughout, Southern thinking has been remarkably self-
conscious, or rather region-conscious; the South has thought
about itself consistently and constantly.

What is it thinking about now? The same thing—itself.
It is thinking about its immediate problems in four main
fields—race relations, labor relations, politics and industrialization. As usual, it is thinking, not because it wants to, but
because it has to.

The radical changes which it is undergoing stimulate
thought. They are summed up in the saying: "Cotton has
gone West; livestock has come East; the Negroes have gone
North, and the Yankees have come South." Since November
4, 1952, the Republicans have come South, too.

So the present South is simmering over the fires of muta-
bility. It is concerned with the question of what it will be
and the problem of what it wants to be. What it wants to be
may be quite different from what America wants to be or is.
The South has always had its own ideas of what it wants to
make of itself.

To understand contemporary Southern thought, one has
to dig deep into past Southern thinking. To psychoanalyze
the South, one must go back to the South's adolescence a
century ago—and the South was nothing if not adolescent in
the 1850's.

Yet it had then a fairly clear idea of what it wanted to be.
It set its face against what it considered to be the materialistic, middle-class culture of the North. The South had a
vision of the sort of civilization it desired for itself, if not
for the nation. What value did that vision have then? What,
if any, does it have now?

To answer these questions it is necessary to take a quick
survey of a century of Southern thought.

From 1850 to 1860 Southerners thought mainly about defending slavery and secession as means of preserving an aristocratic civilization—let us call them the Defenders.

From 1860 to 1870 they thought mainly about war and survival—call them the Fighters.

From 1870 to 1900 they thought mainly about how to create law and order out of chaos, how to make the transition from an aristocratic to a democratic form of government, and how to lay the foundations for an economic system which would give Southerners a chance to make a living—call them the Architects.

From 1900 to the present they have thought mainly about the problems left over from the preceding period, and also about how to educate the people and how to create a more excellent civilization on the ruins of the old—call them the Educators, Builders and Gadflies.

Obviously the South thought about those things it was forced to think about, and it had plenty of problems to absorb its thinking power. Thinking was not a popular exercise—the South banished quite a few thinkers whose thought ran counter to the prevailing mental winds, *e.g.*, Hinton R. Helper, Walter Hines Page and James Spencer Bassett—but it was a necessary exercise. Factors stimulating thought were poverty, politics and the challenge of wasted natural and human resources. Factors discouraging thought were pride, complacency, hopelessness, laziness, genteelism, the easygoing habits of rural or small-town life, the premium placed on conformity and the stigma which attached to independent thought.

### *1850–1860*

From 1850 to 1860 the South was forced to think about slavery and secession. The quality of the thinking wasn't nearly as good as it was earlier when Thomas Jefferson described slavery as a system which, "permitting one-half the citizens thus to trample on the rights of the others, transforms those into despots and these into enemies, destroys the morals of the one part and the *amor patriae* of the other. . . . Indeed I tremble for my country when I reflect that God is just." The influence of the upper South was supplanted by that of the deep South, unfortunately.

The South just prior to the Civil War—the South of slavery, secession and "the purple dream of an America we have not been"—had three outstanding defenders. John C. Calhoun defended it philosophically and politically; Alexander H. Stephens defended it legalistically, and Henry B. Timrod defended it poetically.

Southerners, as well as others, forget what the South stood for, or squeeze the life out of it by compressing it between two narrow, abstract words, "states' rights." They remember the husk but forget the fruit. Yet it was patently something more than "states' rights" which kept Southern men and women fighting, working and praying long after they were undeniably defeated and their civilization was utterly destroyed.

What was that "something"? It was, in brief, the ideal of a Southern utopia, the dream of a civilization which would place the few above the many, excellence above equality, yet which would not desert the democratic form of government.

This ideal of the pre-Civil War South has been described by Vernon L. Parrington in his *Main Currents in American Thought* as "a humane and cultivated democracy, set free from the narrow exactions of economics to engage in the higher work of civilization." One wonders how Southern thinkers thought they could set themselves free of these exactions by ignoring them, but Parrington considered the conception "worthy of the generous Southern mind" and concluded that it "would not suffer by comparison with the Northern dream of an exploitative industrialism."

The Southern thinkers of that time were classicists, and their thinking had two fatal defects: a false assumption that a "humane and cultivated democracy" could be based on slavery; an ever increasing tendency to restrict the greatest good to the smallest number.

Defenders of the Old South assumed that there was no material difference between chattel slavery in the South and what it called wage-slavery in the North, or that, if there were a difference, it was all in favor of the South. Southern writing of the time was full of reminders of how Southern masters and mistresses took tender care of their slaves, even when they were too old to work, while Northern industrialists cast out their "wage slaves" to starve, freeze and die whenever it became profitable to do so.

John C. Calhoun, strangely enough, looked on slavery as the indispensable foundation of freedom. He supported slavery in the name of liberty. "Many in the South," he asserted, "once believed that it [slavery] was a moral and political evil. That folly and delusion are gone. We see it now in its true light, and regard it as the most safe and stable basis for free institutions in the world."

How did Calhoun get that way? This amazing feat of rationalization by one of the greatest logicians in American history was accomplished by means of an ingenious mental process, which went somewhat as follows:

Democracy is possible only among equals, as ancient history proves; inequality between economic classes, the exploiter and the exploited, has always prevented the successful functioning of democracy; industrialism has created classes in the North and made true democracy impossible there; in the South, on the contrary, there is only one class, that of free and equal whites (the Negro didn't count); Athens and other ancient democracies subsisted on slave labor; such labor is necessary to give the ruling class sufficient time and opportunity to create a fine civilization; therefore the South offers the only chance in America for a "humane and cultivated democracy" of equals.

Why then was there no mass migration of Northern workers Southward to take advantage of the pure democracy of the South? The South did not stop to ask itself that question.

When John Adams asked Calhoun whether liberty, justice, the rights of man and the Declaration of Independence meant nothing at all, Calhoun simply replied that those rights were just but that they applied in the South only to the white race, that furthermore slavery was "the best guarantee of equality among the whites, producing an unvarying equality among them," and that "with us the two great divisions of society are not the rich and the poor, but the black and the white."

Many people in the South believed this, but that did not make it so. Calhoun doubtless believed it in the heat of oratory, but it would have been difficult for him to convince a poor white man, who could enter the plantation mansion of the wealthy slaveholder only by the back door, that there was any truth in it. Calhoun's fanciful picture of a one-class white South was utterly at variance with the fact.

The second fundamental defect of the Southern system was this very thing. It bred inequality among whites. When we ask ourselves what was wrong with the Southern dream of a society which would flower in independence, honor, courage, generosity, hospitality, harmony, magnanimity, statesmanship, literature and art, the answer is simple. It left out of account the bulk of the Southern people—the 5,000,000 whites who did not own slaves. Slavery, far from being the "best guarantee of equality," was in fact the surest guarantee of inequality. There were, it is true, nonslaveholding whites in the hill country of the South who were educated and fairly well off, since they met little competition from slave labor, but in the South in general the slave system kept nonslaveholding whites in perpetual bondage to ignorance and poverty.

Every Southern dream has its gadfly, and the gadfly for the dream of Calhoun and Timrod was named Hinton Rowan Helper. He punctured the bubble when he wrote *The Impending Crisis* in 1857. Its theme may be grasped in the following excerpt:

"As a general rule poor white persons are regarded with less esteem and attention than Negroes; and though the condition of the latter is wretched beyond description, vast numbers of the former are infinitely worse off. . . . The lords of the lash are not only absolutely masters of the blacks . . . but they are also the orators and arbiters of all nonslaveholding whites, whose freedom is merely nominal and whose unparalleled illiteracy is purposely and fiendishly perpetuated."

This book made its author a hated Helper indeed. It influenced Lincoln, became a Republican campaign document, and attained an immense circulation for that time. Brilliant, fearless and inspired by the purest love of his region, Helper attained while a young man a degree of infamy which few villains have been able to achieve after long lives devoted to all manner of iniquities. He became the most hated man in the South, at a time when hatred grew to full stature. His fellow countrymen whom he tried to aid referred to him in their milder moments as "that vile wretch Helper."

Helper was interested in what he called the "niggerless" whites, and he was almost the only American who was. While Northern abolitionists were bemoaning the fate of the slaves, Helper was bemoaning that of the slaveless Southern whites. He saw that slavery was worse on them than it was on the slaves themselves. He recognized the fact that slave labor discouraged free labor, that it ate up the capital which otherwise would have been available for the establishment of industries, that consequently the poor white man of the South, unlike his brother in the North, had no hope of acquiring wealth or education but was condemned by the plantation economy to a life of poverty and ignorance. "Indeed," he wrote, "the unprofitableness of slavery is a monstrous evil, when considered in all its bearing; it makes us poor, poverty makes us ignorant, ignorance makes us wretched, wretchedness makes us wicked, and wickedness leads to the devil."

Helper aspired to be the voice of the five million forgotten men of the South. He did become their voice, but they could not hear him. He had the misfortune to write a book for a class who could not read.

The class which could read outlawed his book, naturally enough, as "incendiary literature," which it certainly was, and made it a felony to circulate it (see the North Carolina criminal code of that day). The first offense was punishable by imprisonment of not less than a year and a public whipping. The second was punishable by death. The theory was that such books would incite rebellion among the slaves, although it is difficult nowadays to see how it could have done this: in the first place, the slaves couldn't read it, and in the second place, if they had read it they would have learned that they were better off than the nonslaveholding whites. Southerners in those days, however, were in no mood to make fine, logical distinctions. Helper was to experience the truth of what another Tar Heel author was to express some fourscore years later in five words, *You Can't Go Home Again.*

The Southern dream ran counter to the whole genius of America when it tried to found freedom on slavery and it ran counter to common sense when it attempted to base democracy on inequality. In sum the South was like the little girl who had a curl in the middle of her forehead; when it was good it was very, very good, and when it was bad it was horrid.

### *1860–1870*

From 1860 to 1870 the South thought about war and survival, in so far as it had time or cause to think. War is more a matter of reflex action than cerebration. It is a process in which the blunders of one side match or overmatch those on the other side. Fletcher Pratt in his *Ordeal By Fire,* a seaman's-eye view of land warfare, says: "Military strategy is an art of immense and infantile simplicity." The Civil War was a test of the South's courage and fortitude, not its brains. The South lost the war, but the nation lost the loyal opposition which had served to keep it from going to materialistic extremes.

The Old South firmly believed it had something worth living and dying for, and it did. It fought a war to determine whether its conception of civilization would survive, and it lost. Thenceforth, Americans, being good sports, not only abided by the result of the war but convinced themselves that the Southern way of life had nothing worth preserving and that the Northern way alone had value, because everything was for the best in the best of all possible worlds.

This viewpoint was challenged by a large number of unreconstructed rebels and a small number of stubborn thinkers. Parrington put in his dissent to the course of American history after 1865 when he said that the Lost Cause carried down to defeat more than slavery, that the nation lost with it the idea of decentralized democracy and individual liberty, and that it hurried down the path of "an unquestioning and uncritical consolidation" which placed the power of the state in the hands of the new industrialism. "In the world of Jay

Cooke and Commodore Vanderbilt, the transcendental dream was as much of a lost cause as the plantation dream. . . . A new culture . . . was to dispossess the old culture with its lingering concern for distinction and its love of standards."

So the nation moved all the way from "Emersonian optimism to Dreiserian pessimism."

"The artist," Parrington concluded, "is in revolt, the intellectual is in revolt, the conscience of America is in revolt."

This was a serious charge, couched in harsh words, but anyone who looks at American literature of the twentieth century will see that it is justified.

The intensity, breadth and duration of the revolt are strikingly obvious. Almost all the serious "creative" writers in recent American literature have joined in this revolt, as even a random roll call will indicate: Frank Norris, Stephen Crane, Theodore Dreiser, Sinclair Lewis, H. L. Mencken, James Branch Cabell, Edgar Lee Masters, Sherwood Anderson, Edgar Arlington Robinson, Robinson Jeffers, T. S. Eliot, Dorothy Parker, Ring Lardner, William Faulkner, Thomas Wolfe, Scott Fitzgerald, Erskine Caldwell, John Dos Passos, James Farrell, Norman Mailer, and so on and so on; the Dead-Sea fruits of materialism are, of course, the theme of *The Death of A Salesman, The Hucksters* and *Point of No Return.*

In brief, American writers, severely questioning the values of their culture, finally came to the dark tower of cynicism and suspected that those values—the long, hard pull to the vice presidency of the company, the boiled shirt and the membership in the second-best country club—were superficial or nonexistent.

This disillusionment may not be exactly subversive, but it is a far cry from the early days of this century when Horatio

Alger was a best-selling author. The American fiction cycle
has done a lot of cycling since that time—all the way from
*Jed The Poorhouse Boy* and *Sink Or Swim* to *The Hucksters*
and *Point of No Return*. Thus it has moved from uncritical
acceptance of money-making as an end in itself to a caricature
(if only a slight one) of the American businessman, and
thence to the basic question: what is the end and aim of the
businessman's life?

No way has been discovered, thank heaven, to prevent men
from wondering about such things. Fiction, being in its
higher reaches a rather philosophic art, is interested in standards and values in a materialistic culture, though it treats
the problem involved tangentially, whereas R. H. Tawney
poses it explicitly in his *Religion and the Rise of Capitalism:*

"Agreement as to ends implies the acceptance of a standard
of values. . . . Such a standard must obviously take account
of economic possibilities. But it can not itself be merely
economic, since the comparative importance of economic and
other interests . . . is precisely the point on which it is
needed to throw light. It must be based on some conception
of the requirements of human nature as a whole . . ."

Man's perversely one-track mind ordinarily prevents him
from recognizing these requirements and judging fairly
among them. Thus the Orient throughout history and the
Europe of the Middle Ages overstressed the spiritual side of
man's nature, but modern times are lopsidedly materialistic.
Religion, philosophy and art have very largely given way to
science, politics and economics. Only in rare periods—in
China at certain times, in Renaissance Europe, in Periclean
Athens—have "the requirements of human nature as a whole"
received sufficient justice to make the production of complete men at all likely.

In the 1850's Southern thinkers were trying, however mis-
takenly, to create a civilization which would fashion such

men through a harmony of spiritual and material forces.

The Southern way of life reached its "point of no return" in the 1860's. Greed, class consciousness and class government precluded harmony and magnanimity. The system did promote goodness and fineness, but it limited them to too small a number of owners; it had the instability of a pyramid standing on its apex. To the graces of a Sidney the Old South added the blindness of a Samson. Doubtless the Old South, which had as its guiding light "the greatest good to the smallest number," got what was coming to it when it was destroyed by the greater number. Nevertheless, a barrenly materialistic culture which, while multiplying goods, somehow contrives to bring "the smallest good to the greatest number" may not be the ultimate answer.

If the American way of life is approaching this point, as many of its best writers seem to have assumed of late, perhaps it might be worth while to look back to the Old South in order to see whether it had any values worthy of survival and adoption.

## *1870–1900*

From 1870 to 1900 the South in order to survive had to accomplish three tremendous tasks, any one of which would have been enough to absorb the physical and mental energy of a country in full health and vigor.

First, the South had to create government, to re-establish rudimentary law and order, and supplant the chaos of carpetbag rule with representative government. To do this it had to use three gimmicks which no good people should have had to employ—the Red Shirts, the Ku Klux Klan and the Grandfather Clause. But the South did use them and did establish government. The Red Shirts accomplished by open threats what the Klan accomplished by secret violence. The Grandfather clause was a provision exempting those whose grandfathers could vote from laws preventing illiterates from voting. The result was that illiterate Negroes were prevented from voting but not illiterate whites.

Second, the South had to do something no other part of the country has had to do—it had to change its form of government, root and branch; not a superficial change of administration or parties but a radical change of its whole tradition and philosophy of government, from an aristocratic to a democratic form. This it did or is still doing.

Third, the South simultaneously had to lay the foundation for changing its economy from an almost totally agrarian form to one which would eventually balance agriculture with industry.

While the South was straining every muscle, nerve and brain cell to accomplish these three tasks—which sound as if they must have come straight out of Greek mythology or *Grimm's Fairy Tales*—it found itself in its moments of leisure looking backward with longing to the good old days "befo' the war," the golden era of Southern power and pride.

George W. Cable, Thomas Nelson Page, Mary Noailles Murfree, James Lane Allen, and a host of lesser writers now mercifully forgotten, helped Southerners forget their tribulations by means of novels glorifying the Southern past.

But the South of the last third of the last century was not to be allowed to cross the river and rest in the shade of romance. Every time it took evasive action it was brought back to the row it had to hoe by a home-grown gadfly. As Thomas Nelson Page was chief romanticist of the period, Walter Hines Page was chief gadfly.

Walter Hines Page, who had been educated "up North" —anyway, as far North as Johns Hopkins at Baltimore—and who had worked on the *New York World,* came back home, full of vim and vinegar, to Raleigh, North Carolina to run a

newspaper and to wake the South and civilize her in spite
of herself. With him the South turned over a new page.

On the train coming down from New York, in 1883, he
was hit hard by sights he had forgotten for a spell, and so he
wrote:

"Here was poverty—a depressed population, the idle
squalor of the Negro, now that slavery was relaxed, and the
hopeless inertia of the white man who had been deadened by
an old economic error. . . ."

But Page's energetic optimism immediately got the better
of him, as it always did, and so he wrote of the red hills and
pine barrens passing in review:

"They once bred men; they shall breed men again! And
at last a patient pride swelled up in me that I too was a part
of this land, had roots deep in it, felt it, understood it, believed in it as men who had come into life elsewhere could
not."

This combination of irritation, vision and patriotism in a
young newspaper editor-publisher portended explosions beneath the masthead; they were not long coming.

Page's Southern public enemies were the old and tired
Bourbons who, by reason of ancestry and war record, had
grasped the reins of political or business power and then let
them fall over the dashboard while they dozed off.

Straight-way Page entered into a one-man feud with the
whole lot of them which lasted longer than he lasted in the
South—a couple of years. He had a word for these lethargic
leaders—"mummies"—and he wrote from New York, to which
he returned as refugee, a series of newspaper articles which
he called "The Mummy Letters":

"It is an awfully discouraging business to undertake to
prove to a mummy that it is a mummy. . . .

"Even with our material advancement of late years, there

is no appreciation of scholarship, no chance for intellectual growth.

". . . every movement is balked by the dead weight of these provincial and ignorant men, who are suffered to rule by heredity and by their general respectability in private life—there is absolutely no chance for ambitious men of ability, proportionate to their ability.

"We have a state and a people second in capacity to none in the Union . . . yet . . . the presumptuous powers of ignorance, heredity, decayed respectability and stagnation that control public action and public expression are absolutely leading us backward intellectually. If any is offended, him have I described."

Plenty were offended. They let him know it in various and not ineffective ways.

But a young lawyer in Goldsboro, North Carolina wrote him:

"Fully three-fourths of the people are with you and wish you Godspeed in your efforts to arouse better work, greater fight and activity, and a freer expression of opinions in this State."

The writer of this letter was Charles B. Aycock who, not long afterward, as the "educational Governor" of North Carolina, had a chance to test and to prove the truth of his remarks.

By 1900 Southerners had laid the necessary foundations, in government and economics, for existence. Having concluded that the South would live, they turned their minds to consideration of what sort of life the South wanted.

Early in this period two new factors appeared. The first was a fresh vision of what the South might become. This vision was concerned not with the resurrection of the Old South but the creation of the New South.

It was something more practical than a dream of a Greek

revival and it rested broadly on a new-found faith in democracy which slowly but surely permeated the South.

Charles B. Aycock, who was elected Governor of North Carolina in 1901, expressed this new faith eloquently to a hostile Democratic state convention in 1904. What he said he directed to his own state, but it applied to the South and expressed a feeling that was growing throughout the region.

"This administration has spent much money and it is glad of it. It undoubtedly appears cheaper to neglect the aged, the feeble, the infirm, the defective, to forget the children of this generation, but the man who does it is cursed of God, and the state that permits it is certain of destruction."

This was the voice of the new "humane democracy" in the South. It was certainly a far cry from the Old South with its aristocratic-oligarchic leadership which took little thought of the average man and evinced no pride in him or care for him.

This call to faith in the democratic state was carried on by others, among them Dr. Clarence Poe, son-in-law of Aycock and editor of *The Progressive Farmer*. Dr. Poe in an address to the North Carolina Literary and Historical Association in 1915 quoted Gilbert Chesterton, " 'Men did not love Rome because she was great. She was great because men loved her.' " And Dr. Poe added: "Even so men will not love the North Carolina of tomorrow because she is great. She will be great because her sons and daughters love and have loved her—and loving her give their lives to her enrichment. . . ."

The second important factor in Southern progress was a faith in public education as an immense lever to move the South upward and forward. Many Southern leaders came to believe that the South could attain a better way of life only by a combination of education and industry, culture and commerce.

The South took to heart the saying, "What you want in

the region, you must put in the schools; and what you want
in the schools, you must put in the teacher." In this period
many of its ablest young men went into teaching, because
that profession offered the most patriotic outlet for their
talents; the unfortunate sequel was that all but a few left it,
for the reason that they could not make a living in it.

One of the most inspired and persuasive advocates of education as the South's prime need was Edward Kidder Graham, Sr., who was president of the University of North
Carolina when he died at the age of forty-three during the
First World War. He interpreted anew the function of the
University in the State. When he came to office, the University of North Carolina and the denominational colleges in
the State had been carrying on a foolish and apparently
interminable feud which was largely caused by the difficulties, in a poverty-ridden state, of getting funds for any sort
of higher education. Graham put the whole matter on a
higher, more realistic and fruitful plane when he expressed
the truth that the University "recognizes no antagonist . . .
but ignorance. Ignorance it conceives as the unpardonable
sin in a democracy."

He proposed to make the University of North Carolina
campus state-wide in service to the people and he thought of
its extension division, "not as thinly stretching out its resources to the state boundaries for the purposes of protective
popularity, or as carrying down to those without the castle
gates broken bits of learning, but as the radiating power of a
new passion, carrying in natural circulation the unified culture of the race to all parts of the body politic." The purpose
of higher education, as he saw it, was the production of
"masterful, intelligent men, eternally and invincibly loyal
to their highest natures," and he had no use for the college or
university which had reached the point where "success in the
things for which it stands no longer appeals to those within

it." He concluded that the university's reason for existence
is "to liberate the ideal as a fighting force in the common
affairs of men; and in these terms the American university
will give effective answer to the nation's fateful question:
What in the way of clear guidance have you to offer, or must
we look to another?"

Calling on his people to abandon a policy of penuriousness
to education which "had kept the State in ignorance and the
poor in poverty," he contended that full support for education could make his region the "center of the next great forward movement in American progress" and usher in that
gracious commonwealth just beyond the boundaries of the
visible "for which men have dreamed and died, but scarcely
dared to hope."

His words were not wasted. His faith, expressed so force-
fully forty years ago, gave the University of North Carolina
the momentum which still carries it forward. Aycock made
his state conscious of its need for public education; Graham,
of its need for higher education.

One significant thing about the period from 1900 to about
1930 is that the gadflies had come, not into power perhaps,
but certainly into prominence. They had faith in the South's
capabilities but they dwelt on its deficiencies.

The South was not yet ready to suffer gadflies gladly.
Walter Hines Page said sorrowfully from his editorial sanc-
tuary in New York, "I shall some day buy a house where I
was not allowed to work for one and be laid away in the soil
that I love. I wanted to work for the old State; it had no use
for me, it seems."

And James Spencer Bassett, historian and professor at
Trinity College (now Duke University) in Durham, North
Carolina, found the South too hot to handle shortly after he
wrote in an article in the *South Atlantic Quarterly* (a schol-
arly publication of Trinity College) in 1903:

"Now Booker T. Washington is a great and good man, a Christian statesman, and take him for all in all the greatest man, save General Lee, born in the South in a hundred years."

Dr. Bassett later revealed that he inserted this sentence in his article, which was prophetically entitled "Stirring the Fires of Race Antipathy," in order to attract attention to the young and struggling *South Atlantic Quarterly* of which he was editor. It did.

It also attracted attention to Dr. Bassett. Southerners, of course, overlooked the point of the article which was to show that Booker T. Washington "is not a typical Negro . . . He is an exceptional man . . . It is therefore too much to hope for a continued appearance of such men in the near future."

Multitudes of Southerners were infuriated by a comparison which placed a Negro on a plane with General Lee and above their own fathers and grandfathers; they demanded Dr. Bassett's removal from the faculty. The trustees and faculty of Trinity College rallied in the name of academic freedom to Gadfly Bassett's defense and turned down all efforts to oust him. But Bassett did not remain long in a Southern environment which had shown itself so hostile toward him. He, too, went North.

### *1930–1953*

The period from 1930 to the present may be described as the Golden Age of the Gadflies. Great swarms of them hovered all over the region from Virginia to Texas; the South, like the white heifer, Io, who in human form incurred Hera's wrath as Zeus' mistress, bounded wildly before their stings, but mainly along the road of progress.

These gadflies were of two main species—the sociological-research gadfly and the literary gadfly—and they ranged all

the way from Howard W. Odum to William Faulkner and
from Calvin B. Hoover to Lillian Smith.

The research gadflies wore horn-rimmed spectacles and carried yardsticks with them; their principal hive or habitat was
the Chapel Hill-Durham area, and the Southern economy
was their target.

Their names include those of Howard W. Odum, Rupert
B. Vance, Harriet Herring, Samuel H. Hobbs, Jr., William
T. Couch, Calvin B. Hoover and B. U. Ratchford. The research departments of the Federal Reserve Bank, particularly
at Richmond and Atlanta, also have done excellent work
along this line.

As the Oracle of Delphi said to Socrates, "Know thyself!"
so the research gadflies of the South said it to their region.
Thanks to them, the South has been thinking about itself
keenly, comprehensively, copiously, courageously and objec-
tively, so that the South today knows more about itself—its
resources, advantages, deficiencies and needs—than any other
section of the country knows about itself.

However, it was in the field of Southern literature that
America witnessed such an outpouring of gadflies as it had
never seen before and probably will not see again.

Some of these gadflies were like wasps; they had friction in
their fiction; they had stings in their tales. Of such were
William Faulkner, Thomas Wolfe and Erskine Caldwell, to
name only three.

Another species were like honey bees, gathering the honey
of the Old South in books and stinging the New South into a
sense of shame by contrast. Of such were William Alexander
Percy, Archibald Rutledge and Stark Young. Their stained-
glass sentences transmitted something of the honor, grace and
glory of the Old South, but left out the darker phases.

Still another species of Southern writers, notably Paul
Green as author of *The Lost Colony* and Inglis Fletcher as

author of the Carolina Series, sought to remind the South of
its origins in Renaissance England and thus inspire it to
reach a hand through time to catch something of the vision,
energy, versatility, courage and magnificence which the age
of Elizabeth and Raleigh represents, which our age needs and
which is a rightful and precious part of the South's heritage.

So the answer to the question, "What is the South thinking?" is that it is thinking a lot about itself. As evidence note
these works which came out between 1930 and 1940:

*I'll Take My Stand* (1930), the manifesto of the Southern
agrarians of Tennessee as part of "the pastoral rebellion of
the earth against machines, against the Age of Steam."

*Southern Regions* (1936), Howard W. Odum's monumental work which held a mirror up to Southern resources
and deficiencies.

*Report on Economic Conditions of the South* (1938). This
report was made to President Franklin D. Roosevelt by the
National Emergency Council aided by "an advisory committee of Southern citizens known for their interest in the region
and their familiarity with its problems." They ranged from
Barry Bingham, publisher of the Louisville *Courier Journal,*
to Miss Lucy Randolph Mason, CIO representative of Atlanta, Georgia, and from Gen. John C. Persons, president of
the First National Bank of Birmingham, Alabama, to H. L.
Mitchell, secretary-treasurer of the Tenant Farmers Union,
Memphis, Tennessee. President Roosevelt in his acceptance
of the report called the South "the nation's number one
economic problem."

The report, which stressed Southern defects and needs, hit
the South in the face as squarely as H. L. Mencken's "Sahara
of the Bozart" did some twenty years before, and it did for
the South in the economic field what Mencken's article did

in the cultural field; it waked the South up and set it to work to disprove what had been alleged against it.

The report dealt with various Southern problems, including low per capita income, absentee ownership of industries, farm tenancy, education, health and housing. Its findings may be roughly summed up as follows:

The South, despite its resources, is poor in the machinery for converting these to the uses of its people. "Its potentialities have been neglected and its opportunities unrealized. . . . Lacking industries of its own, the South has been forced to trade the richness of its soil, its minerals and forests, and the labor of its people for goods manufactured elsewhere. If the South received such goods in sufficient quantity to meet its needs it might consider itself adequately paid . . .

"Northern producers and distributors are losing profits and Northern workers are losing work because the South cannot afford to buy their goods."

Rupert B. Vance, author of *The Human Geography of the South,* carried forward this line of thought by proving that the South has a duty to be prosperous and that it owes this duty not only to itself but also to the whole nation. "The nation should come to realize," wrote Dr. Vance in a booklet entitled *Wanted: The South's Future for the Nation* (1946), "that in the long run further industrialization of the South will aid, not injure, the national well-being. The South, in its turn, should recover from its low-wage complex and realize that a rising level of wages in the area will create greater markets and increased well-being. This, it should be realized, applies also to the Negro, who has the lowest level of living of any large group in America."

What was Southern thought, in this rich but hitherto neglected field of economics, trying to do? To utilize Southern resources and to bring the South back into the Union as an equal member.

What progress is the South making toward this goal?

In 1948, ten years after the *Report on the Economic Conditions of the South* appeared, it was plain that the South had made progress in the absolute sense of the word. It was certainly making more money and living better than it ever had done before. Whatever may be said against the New Deal, it did improve the lot of the poor, and the South had more than its share of those.

But was the South making more progress than the rest of the country? This much could be said: the South was closing the gap. If per capita income is any indication, the South was making progress at a faster rate than the rest of the country:

> 1938, average per capita income in the South $315
> 1938, average per capita income in the nation $604
> 1948, average per capita income in the South $797
> 1948, average per capita income in the nation $1150

If a longer period is taken for comparison, it will be noted that from 1929 to 1952, while the per capita income rose 111 per cent in the nation, it rose 179 per cent in the South.

Editor Johnathan Daniels, of the Raleigh, North Carolina *News and Observer,* however, suspected that Southern progress—national too, for that matter—was not all it was cracked up to be, and he cited as evidence more holes in the roads at a time when more cars were on them, and more teachers who felt poorer and so went into other work at a time when there were more and more children who needed to be taught. He feared that if the South learned that in terms of comparative progress it was "only a little way from the point at which it began," such a discovery could be "the basis of despair."

Doubtless it could, but hope, not despair, has been the mood of the modern South. Events since 1940 have seen a steady gain for the South in material things. The South is still behind the rest of the country, but its rate of climb is faster. If the South ever came to the time when it had fewer problems than the rest of the nation it wouldn't recognize itself.

## Contemporary Thought

What is the South thinking about now?

Four broad fields in which it is thinking hard—as usual, not because it wants to but because it has to—are race relations, labor relations, politics and industrialization.

In race relations the South is ready to give the Negro a fairer chance and more equal opportunity in various matters, including education, politics and industry. The number of Negroes who vote is increasing rapidly; quite a few Southern cities employ Negro policemen and some have elected Negro councilmen. In industry the absorption of the white labor supply will perforce open up new opportunities for Negro labor if industrial expansion continues. In higher education the recent growth of Negro colleges and universities has been phenomenal; fifty years ago there were in the South only a few Negro colleges with few students in attendance, whereas now there are ninety-two Negro colleges with more than 62,000 students; the Negro colleges in North Carolina have, in the past few years, far outstripped the white colleges in rate of growth and increase of appropriations; they had further to go, but this increase of higher education for Negroes is genuine and, despite variations, is South-wide. Public education for Negroes has had a similar increase; a good deal of it is due to the courts and the educational foundations, but much has come about through the South's belated recognition of the truth of Booker T. Washington's saying that you can't keep a man in the gutter without getting down there with him.

However, the South is not ready to abandon segregation in

public education, for fear of the destructive effect which mixed schools might have on a state's educational system. The South is therefore looking for a political gimmick to serve it as effectively in staving off mixed schools as the Grandfather Clause did in restoring workable government a generation or so ago. The amendment of the Constitution of South Carolina to delete the provision making public education mandatory is evidence of the lengths the South may be prepared to go.

Race relations in the South may be as difficult as ever, but not as violent as they were.

The South is thinking about labor relations, although not as much as one might judge by the wordage expended on the problem. Most of the argument, of course, is the result of reflex action rather than thought; a good deal of management in the South still tends to look on labor unions as deadly weapons, while labor generally considers them useful and beneficent institutions. There has been a big change in the attitude of management and the public toward organized labor in the South; a labor union *per se* is no longer put in the category of black magic. It may even be favorably received by the public as a useful tool in lifting a per capita income which is admitted to be dangerously low.

The South is thinking about politics—certainly nothing unusual. But the subject matter is more complicated now than it was in the good old days when the choice between Republican and Democrat was the choice between black and white. Today the South seems to be foregoing its traditional allegiance to the Democratic party. It may be too early to say for sure, but the "Solid South" looked more like a gas than a solid in 1952. Or it may be comparable to a radio-active substance, such as U-235, with states shooting off the hitherto indivisible Democratic atom into Republican outer darkness.

Is the South deserting the Democratic party or vice versa? It is hard to tell. Patently the old gray Democratic party ain't what she used to be. The new Democratic party somehow became what the old Republican party was—the party of big government, big spending and the Negro—while the Republican party under President Eisenhower seems to be the party of states' rights.

One thing which may be said with assurance, however, is that the South is gradually forgetting its old grievances against the Republicans, although it is true that the GOP could furnish some new ones overnight. As it is, freight rates are being equalized; the tariff means less and less to a South which is being swiftly industrialized, and while the tragic era of Reconstruction is fading from memory, the corruption which fastened on Washington in the Truman Administration makes the Democratic party look more carpet-baggerish to some Southerners today than the Republican party does.

So Southern political thinking may be diagnosed as "confused."

The South is thinking about industrialization. The South has at least 80 per cent of the nation's cotton textile industry, it is getting practically all of the new chemical fiber industry, and it is reaching out for the woolen-worsted and textile-machinery manufacturing industries. In addition, the paper and pulp industry, the chemical industry, the makers of electric appliances, arms, clothing, drugs, et cetera, are coming South in force. Among inducements which the South offers industry are raw materials, good climate, cheap power, plentiful factory sites and a surplus of labor "willing to give a full day's work for a full day's wages." The South is competing successfully for industry on the move, and the Southern states are competing keenly among themselves for it.

At the same time Southern agriculture is being mechanized. What held it back so long—cheap hand labor—is no longer an indispensable part of the picture. The Southern farmer today is making machinery do efficiently what mules and cheap labor used to do inefficiently. Research and invention have transformed many farms from places of unprofitable drudgery to something more closely resembling profitable industrial establishments. Some of the factors responsible for this are the mechanical cotton picker, chemical weed killers and flame throwers, crop dusting by airplanes, new types of disease-resistant seeds, soil improvers such as Krilium, artificial insemination, new cultivators and harvesters. It all means more efficiency and profits.

The point is that the South is changing fast. It is becoming something new because something new has been added—industry. The South was rural, agrarian, easy-going, poor, and proud of its distinctive way of life. Now it is becoming urban, industrial, hard-working, comparatively prosperous and relatively standardized. At any rate, that is what it will soon become if it follows Newton's first law of motion, "A body set in motion tends to remain in motion," and does not consciously and energetically exert its will to direct its growth and become what it wants to become. If it does not make that effort, the South will follow the iron rails of the road of least resistance laid down for it by its new industrial revolution to the station at the end of the line, called "Standardization."

# PART IV

---

## WHAT IS THE SOUTH BECOMING?

# 14

## The Almost Irresistible Force

---

When the almost irresistible force of industrialization meets the not quite immovable object of the Southern way of life, what happens?

The South will move in a new direction. Where to, is another question.

Clearly the South is simmering over the fires of mutation. It is becoming more industrialized and less plantationized, more urban and less rural, more standardized and less individualized, more American and less Southern.

Yet there is a large measure of resistance to these changes. There is something in the age of industrialization which is antipathetic to the Southern spirit. The South resists being made over in the image of the North or West. What it will become in the end depends not only on material factors but also on what it wants to make of itself.

"Industrialization" is here used merely as a handy label, but it is in truth too narrow and simple a word for the vast, powerful and complex force which is at work on the South. That force is composed of four main elements—the economic, the educational, the political and the cultural. The trend of all these is in the same direction, and they interact on one another, each pushing the others onward; therefore, the force is greater than the sum of its parts.

The industrialization of the South is proceeding at such a rapid rate that it amazes the South itself.

During the years 1951 and 1952 the South added an average of one new multimillion dollar industrial plant per day to its economy. Diversification is the new order. To its old stand-bys such as textiles and tobacco, the South is adding a variety of new industries such as the manufacturing of paper, petroleum and chemical products. There is a strong and increasing movement of industry from the North to the South. Much of this consists of small or medium-sized plants, but some of it is big stuff. Du Pont builds a $17,000,000 orlon plant at Camden, South Carolina. Southland Paper Mills locates a $30,000,000 paper manufacturing concern at Lufkin, Texas. General Electric constructs a $25,000,000 transformer plant at Rome, Georgia, and a $200,000,000 electrical appliance manufactory near Louisville, Kentucky, where more than 15,000 workers will be employed.

The significant point is that the South has been consistently running ahead of the rest of the country in increase of wages paid and value added by manufacturing.

The main reasons for the South's rapid rate of industrialization are not obscure. They may be summed up in three *M*'s: materials, men and markets.

The South is as usual a gigantic producer of raw materials. It grows 100 per cent of the nation's sugar cane, peanuts and tung oil; 95 per cent of its cotton, tobacco and sweet potatoes; 78 per cent of its rice, and 42 per cent of its citrus fruits. It produces 100 per cent of its bauxite and sulphur; 95 per cent of its phosphate rock; 75 per cent of its natural gas; 60 per cent of its petroleum, and 50 per cent of its bituminous coal.

Manpower available for industry is the second great drawing card in the South's industrialization. Because of its high birth rate, the South usually has a big surplus of farm labor which normally goes North to the factories to make a living. Now the factories are coming South to the labor at a time when increasing mechanization on the farm is freeing more and more farm labor for other work. By 1956, it is estimated, the trend from mules to machines on Southern farms will displace 2,000,000 farm workers, but those who remain will produce two and a half times what the South produced on its farms in 1943. Industry, tired of scraping the bottom of the manpower barrel in the North, is moving South to get the labor where the labor is, and it has found this labor to be steady and intelligent, tractable and trainable.

The third big ingredient is the vast new market for manufactured products which has been created by the new buying power inherent in the new wages.

Other factors of prime importance in the South's industrialization are lower costs, research and education.

"We moved to get lower costs," said a spokesman for a woolen manufacturing company which moved from New England to North Carolina. "For labor, taxes, workmen's compensation, every element of cost but raw wool, will be lower than in Massachusetts." Costs of land, power, water and fuel are likely to be lower, too.

Education on the public-school level is providing a supply of literate labor which is relatively new in the South. Vocational education and the acquisition of various trades and skills by Southerners in the armed services increase the effectiveness of Southern labor. And in many colleges and universities, courses in business administration are turning out bright young men who are trained in the fundamentals of management, industrial and commercial.

There is evidence that, while the migration of educated persons from the South continues, the net results of population shifts now actually favor the South, with more of the people who are well educated and hold responsible positions coming into the South than are going out.

Thus all things seem to work together for the propagation of industry in the South.

It is, then, no wonder that glowing prophecies have been made of the South's future. Ernest E. Norris, president of the Southern Railway, described the South as "the most promising piece of real estate in the nation." David Lilienthal, former chairman of the Tennessee Valley Authority, asserted a few years ago: "The South is the number one region of the United States, and economic progress here within the next twenty years will be the greatest the nation has ever seen." Dean Paul W. Chapman of the University of Georgia, in concluding a series of articles on all the Southern states, wrote in 1951: "Regardless of whatever gains are ahead, the South will outgain the nation."

The ramifications of the South's industrialization are almost endless, but its favorable effects are obvious in these fields: capital, race relations, politics and culture.

Capital is "wealth used in producing more wealth." For half a century or more the South was so lacking in capital with which to finance large business ventures that it felt, and generally was, industrially impotent; it therefore resorted to selling its "profit sites" to outside capital. It is still doing so, with the alluring stimulus of state advertisements aimed at attracting new industry. But the South is also amassing capital at a rapid rate. Not all of the profits of outside capital go back where the money came from; a good deal of it is plowed back into Southern real estate. And of course wages and salaries paid in the South tend to stay in the South. Increasingly, the South is financing Southern business with Southern capital, using its new-found wealth to "produce more wealth."

Race relations have improved because the tensions attendant on poverty, including the cutthroat competition between
poor white people and poorer Negroes struggling to live on
a bare subsistence level, have been relaxed in an atmosphere
of relative well-being.

The political climate of the South has become more tem-
perate, too, with a larger measure of wealth more widely dis-
tributed. The diminution, though not the disappearance, of
the Southern demagogue coincides with the diminution of
his "wool-hat" constituents. The men who have nothing to
lose but their grudges and prejudices are becoming a minor-
ity which is dwindling so fast as to render it far more difficult
for unscrupulous mountebanks to rise to political power on
a popular wave of ignorance and resentment. No longer
does a United States Senator from a Southern state find it
politically profitable to threaten to chase a President of the
United States with a pitchfork.

The Institute of Government at Chapel Hill, North Carolina, which links politics and education, is something new
under the sun. It is the creation of Albert Coates, a law professor, and got its start under the administration of President
Frank P. Graham of the University of North Carolina. It is
founded on the safe assumption that most public servants
when elected or appointed to office know very little about
their jobs. The Institute proposes to teach them—all of them
from constables to lawmakers—by various means, including
textbooks, law books, a magazine called *Popular Government,* surveys, conferences, meetings of groups of government
employees, and trouble-shooting teams from the Institute
which visit localities calling for their expert services. The
Institute has immeasurably increased the efficiency of state
and local government in North Carolina, and its practices
have been adopted in other states.

Culture, furthermore, has come South with industrial

wealth, after a prolonged absence due to circumstances beyond the South's control. This factor alone would tend to render the new force practically irresistible to a South which has long held an instinctive distrust of industry.

The South is learning that industry creates wealth and wealth fosters culture. The Medici were bankers. Neither the "wool-hat" boys nor the small independent farmers in the Jeffersonian tradition constitute the foundation on which great universities, art galleries and symphony orchestras flourish. These appear to be a by-product of wealth producing more wealth.

Occasionally the Southern writer raises the question whether "the hum of machinery, the ceaseless rattle of spindle and loom" are so loud that "we are in danger of hearing little else." But most Southerners are coming around to seeing the light that commerce and culture are Siamese twins.

When H. L. Mencken published "Sahara of the Bozart" in 1920, both commerce and culture in the South were at a pretty low ebb. In that meat-ax essay, Mencken sized the South up savagely but with considerable accuracy: "In all that Gargantuan paradise of the fourth-rate, there is not a single picture gallery worth going into, or a single orchestra capable of playing the nine symphonies of Beethoven, or a single opera house, or a single theater devoted to decent plays. Once you have counted James Branch Cabell . . . you will not find a single Southern prose writer who can actually write. . . ."

Some three decades later the "Sahara" is blossoming like the rose. Literature, drama, art and music are all over the place. Since 1900, as Dr. H. W. Odum notes, the South has contributed "no less than 5,000 titles to the full-sized book literature of the nation. . . . Of these approximately one-half may be classified as 'literature' in the traditional sense, with 1,000 volumes of fiction, 500 biographies, 400 poetry and 125 drama. The total 'writing' contributions, however, include 800 volumes of history, 800 on Negro life, 400 on nature and the folk, more than a hundred each on socio-economic studies, nature and resources, travel and description." For whatever it may indicate as to the quality of their literary output, Southerners won in that time eight Pulitzer prizes in the field of the novel, three in drama, three in biography and three in poetry. Ten of the eleven best sellers which exceeded or approximated sales of a million copies were written by Southerners.

Southerners may not read books but they certainly write them.

In theatrical fare, the South, like the rest of the country, gets what nourishment it can from the thin gruel it imports from Hollywood and, occasionally, Broadway.

But significant work in the drama is coming out of the universities and the little theater movement in the South. The Carolina Playmakers at the University of North Carolina have sizable accomplishments to their credit, first under Prof. Frederick H. Koch and later under Prof. Samuel Selden. Among their alumni are playwrights Paul Green, Kermit Hunter, Josephina Niggli and Howard Richardson, not to mention novelists Noel Houston, Max Steele, Betty Smith and Thomas Wolfe. Paul Green in *The Lost Colony, The Common Glory* and *Faith of Our Fathers* developed a new form, the symphonic drama, which utilizes historic outdoor background, music and dancing, reaching a hand through time to catch on stage the spirit which made America great. Kermit Hunter, working on the same model, has dramatized the tragic story of the Cherokee Indians in *Unto These Hills,* which plays during the summers in the reservation in the Great Smoky Mountains National Park, and the early life of

Abraham Lincoln in *Forever This Land* which was produced at New Salem, Illinois.

Other institutions of higher learning in the South which are doing good work in the drama are the University of Miami, the University of Georgia, Tulane University at New Orleans, the Woman's College of the University of North Carolina at Greensboro, and the University of Texas. Other less active but effective groups are located at the University of Virginia, William and Mary College, Rollins College, the University of Alabama, and two Negro schools, Florida A. and M. College and Tennessee A. and I. University.

Community theaters worthy of mention are *Le Petit Théatre du Vieux Carré* which ties in with the Tulane players in New Orleans, the Footlight Players of Charleston, South Carolina, and the little theaters of Atlanta, Macon and Augusta, Georgia; Jacksonville, Tampa, St. Augustine and Ft. Myers, Florida; San Antonio, Dallas and Houston, Texas; Shreveport, Louisiana, and Charlotte, Raleigh and Asheville, North Carolina.

Robert Porterfield's Barter Theater of Abingdon, Virginia, "the first state-subsidized theater in America," is a professional institution which sends out repertory touring companies each fall after a summer stand in the mountains, and which numbers among its alumni Gregory Peck, Hume Cronyn and Jeffrey Lynn.

The state of the theater in the South is spotty. In certain localities there is intensive effort, usually sparked by a university, but most of the South is covered by large open spaces boasting nothing more than high school comedies, amateur minstrel shows, womanless weddings, or polite playmaking by church and club groups.

Nevertheless, the South is waking up, it has made some significant contributions to the national theater and it is on its way.

The South has some fairly good, widely scattered collections of painting and sculpture. Probably the best are at the Isaac Delgado Museum in New Orleans, The High Museum of Art in Atlanta, the Birmingham Art Museum, the Gibbes Art Gallery in Charleston, the Virginia Museum of Fine Art in Richmond, and the John and Mable Ringling Museum of Art in Sarasota, Fla. The Ringling Museum, built in the style of an Italian villa, houses some five hundred paintings which were valued at $50,000,000 in the 1920's and which are said to constitute the best collection of Baroque art in the country.

In Brookgreen Gardens near Georgetown, South Carolina, there is a fine collection of sculpture beautifully displayed in an outdoor setting.

Florida and Texas apparently lead the South in art. "Painters are blossoming like bluebonnets in Texas," according to a Texan. Dallas, Houston and San Antonio have good museums; each year they join to exhibit an all-Texas show of paintings and sculpture.

North Carolina has had an active State Art Society since the 1920's, under the leadership of Mrs. Katherine Pendleton Arrington. The State Art Museum in Raleigh is moving into new quarters in 1954 with $2,000,000 worth of paintings, half coming from the Kress Collection and half having been bought with an appropriation of a million dollars from North Carolina Legislature. Nobody thought the legislature would so invest the taxpayers' money—least of all the legislators themselves—but they were induced to do it by a remarkably persuasive and pertinacious Tar Heel, former Rhodes scholar and lawyer named Robert Lee Humber, author of the Humber resolution on world federation. Even so, the legislators made their appropriation contingent on two things which they were sure would not come to pass: that their million should be matched by another million

raised by Humber's efforts, and that there should be a million lying around unappropriated in the state treasury. But
both did occur, giving North Carolina what will be one of
the outstanding art collections in the South.

Of course, art museums measured in terms of a few millions of dollars are small potatoes compared with the great
museums of the North and Europe, but their proliferation
in the South, together with a multitude of art schools and
galleries housing traveling exhibits, indicates a rapid rise of
art consciousness (and purchasing power) in a region which
until very recently found its art confined almost exclusively
to prewar family portraits and statues of Confederate soldiers
on courthouse squares.

What the South is doing with, by, for—and to—music must
be heard to be believed.

H. L. Mencken was doubtless right when he said some
thirty years ago that there was not an orchestra in the South
capable of playing the nine symphonies of Beethoven. Today, however, there are a good many more than nine Southern cities and communities with orchestras capable of playing
all nine symphonies. There are chamber music groups capable of playing satisfactorily all of his seventeen string
quartets.

At any rate most of the South's larger cities have symphony
orchestras, including New Orleans, Dallas, San Antonio,
Richmond, Atlanta, Louisville, Miami, Houston, Oklahoma
City, Knoxville, Austin, Birmingham, Chattanooga and Charlotte.

A lot of smaller places have them, too: Oak Ridge, Tennessee, for example, has a symphony orchestra conducted by
a chemist. There are regional orchestras, such as that of
central Florida, and state ones, such as that of Virginia. The
Louisville symphony orchestra a few years ago presented a

program in New York City including Boluslav Martinu's *Intermezzo,* Virgil Thompson's *Wheatfield at Noon,* Claude Almand's *John Gilbert: A Steamboat Overture,* and William Schuman's *Judith,* which was written for and danced by Martha Graham; only one of these works had been performed in New York before.

North Carolina has a good symphony orchestra with headquarters in Chapel Hill. Organized and conducted by Dr. Benjamin Swalin, it brings fine music, by bus, boat and other means of transportation, to people in every cove and cranny of the State, from Cape Hatteras to the Cherokee Reservation in the Great Smokies. It has recently toured most of the South, having played in Florida, Alabama, Georgia, South Carolina, Tennessee and Virginia. Supported partly by the State and partly by subscription, it traveled 10,000 miles in 1952 to give 123 concerts. One hundred and forty thousand school children heard these concerts in one year. To watch the children responding to various sorts of music, from a Mozart minuet and a Brahms symphony to *Sourwood Mountain* and *Gum Tree Canoe,* is a heart-moving experience.

In Raleigh, North Carolina, the Grass Roots Opera Company has sprung up; it takes opera, in English translation, without benefit of scenery or costuming, to town and countryside for a guarantee of $60 for a small opera, such as Mozart's *Cosi fan Tutti* up to $110 for a full-sized one, such as Bizet's *Carmen.*

A good deal of American music, of one sort or another, has come out of the South, as witness the Negro spirituals, the blues, jazz. Springing straight from the primary emotions of religion, sex, sadness and joy, this music is warmed by "the heat of life in the handful of dust."

John Powell of Virginia and Lamar Stringfield of North

Carolina are two of many Southern composers who have
fashioned folk music into sophisticated forms.

The South is by nature a singing, fiddling, music-making
region. Innumerable groups of singers and instrumentalists
are springing up all over it, as usual.

What will result from the exposure of Southerners to the
immense mass and variety of music coming to them by way
of radio and phonograph, symphony orchestra and jukebox,
no one can tell. But there are quite a few persons in the
South now—professors, lawyers, insurance agents, taxi driv-
ers, cooks and bottle washers—who will pronounce Brahms
"Brammams" until they get to know you better, when they
will discourse learnedly and excitedly on the beauties of, say,
the fourth movement of Mozart's *Quartet in D Major,
K 575,* or the second movement of Beethoven's *Quartet in E
Flat Major, Opus 127.* It is not yet quite respectable for men
in the South to know much about music, but the beloved
mistress may be taken to wife at almost any time now, "in
the sight of God and in the face of this company."

The fact is that Southerners take to culture as if it were a
long-lost friend, which indeed it is. They agree with the
dictum of Editor J. L. Garvin of the London *Observer* that
"the capitalism of the future must seek to enter into the
service of art and beauty." The South may fear the Yankees
bearing mills, but when industrialization comes bringing
wealth in one hand and culture in the other, the South is in
no mood to put up a last-ditch resistance.

# 15

## The Not Quite Immovable
## Object

The not quite immovable object is, of course,
the Southern way of life. It arises more from instinct than
philosophy; back of it are the ancient traits and ingrained
habits of a people who are notoriously set in their ways.

Suspicion of the Calvinistic-Puritanical-Yankee notion of
"work-for-work's-sake" is one of those traits. A Calhounistic
"wise and masterly inactivity" is more to the Southern taste
as a general rule. When Southerners read the tributes of
Northern poets to work, such as James Russell Lowell's "and
blessed are the horny hands of toil" or Henry Van Dyke's
"the blessing of earth is toil," they doubt whether either
writer had enough callouses on his hands to know what he
was talking about. Such pep talk just makes Southerners
tired; they have to go somewhere and lie down to digest it.
One reason the South loves cotton farming so much is that it
gives them about six months of each year to loaf and invite
their souls. If the soul refuses the invitation, they just loaf.
When Clarence Cason quoted Edgar Guest, "Hold fast!
Work hard, be strong, be true—The future holds a place for

you," he did so with what he believed to be a "devastating sneer," and was astounded to receive a letter from a man in Massachusetts who wanted to know where to get permission to reprint the stuff as an inspiring message for distribution to the children in the public schools.

The South has long had a deep-seated suspicion of industrialization. It wants the fruits of industry, but not the tree. This attitude goes back to Thomas Jefferson, if not further. Southerners have always been convinced that the planter is a nobler work of God than the manufacturer, the farmer than the mill hand. While the Southerner may not remember the exact words which Jefferson used in the *Notes on Virginia* in 1785, the sentiment is bred in his bone:

"Those who labor in the earth are the chosen people of God . . . While we have land to labor then, let us never wish to see our citizens occupied at a work-bench or twirling a distaff. Carpenters, masons, smiths are wanting in husbandry, but, for the general operations of manufacture, let our work-shops remain in Europe. . . . The mobs of great cities add just so much to the support of pure government as sores do to the strength of the human body."

By 1800, it is true, Jefferson had so completely changed his mind about the undesirability of industry that he wrote, "We must now place the manufacturer by the side of the planter," but the South paid no attention to that.

In the 1850's Southerners talked about the evils of capitalism with its "wage-slaves" as bitterly as if they had been Karl Marx and Friedrich Engels, though to be sure it was not the capitalism of the Southern planter but the capitalism of the Northern manufacturer to which they objected.

Even today feudalism is more congenial than industrialism to a good deal of the South which has not yet moved all the way from status to contract. This is the South which not only likes the Negro "in his place" but likes every man in his place and thinks there is a certain place providentially provided for him. To this South, industrialization, with its shift from status to contract and its creation of a new-rich, rootless and pushing class of people, is plainly instigated by the devil.

The Southern farmer still tends to look on himself as a better and freer man than the mill worker. He doesn't mind getting up before daylight—he is used to that—but he resents even the thought of being gotten out of bed by a whistle. He feels that he is his own boss—even when he is a virtual slave to his landlord or supply man—and he can't stand for some stranger to tell him how many hours a day he shall work cooped up in a mill. When poverty drives him off the land into the mill, he considers it a comedown for him to move from Tobacco Road to Mill Village; even the clodhopper looks down on the lint-dodger.

This attitude, which is common to all classes of Southern society, is one of the brakes on the Southern transition from an agrarian toward an industrial economy. If Southerners had been industry-minded, they would have promoted industry and become prosperous long ago, instead of sitting back and ascribing all their ills to the outcome at Gettysburg and Appomattox. Sometimes a Southerner can see this, and sometimes he can't. It depends on the mood he is in. Even the most thoughtful and clear-sighted Southerners have this intermittent blind spot which leads them into queer lapses of logic. For example, Johnathan Daniels, after going to considerable trouble to prove in *A Southerner Discovers the South* that the South's backwardness was caused not so much by the Civil War as by the traits of Southerners themselves, ended his book with this sentiment: "Cato did not ride through Carthage on a train and blame its condition on the Carthaginians. This much only I ask of the Yankees." The explanation doubtless is that while Southerners don't mind

putting the blame on Southerners, they don't want foreigners
getting in that game.

The South has long made a practice of letting sure-fire
money-making schemes slip through its hands or turning
them over to Northern capital for profitable exploitation;
so that those who do not know Southerners may be tempted
to conclude that they hate money. As we know, Dr. Charles
H. Herty of Georgia invented a process for making newsprint from pine trees, but Southerners merely sat back and
hoped that some Northerner would come along and set up
the mill to make the paper, and incidentally the profits.
Shortly before his death, Dr. Herty was asked what he
thought was the matter with the South. He answered that
he had been asking himself that question all his life and still
didn't know. There seems to be something in the statement
that "the conditions of Northern industrialism are oppressive to the Southern nature."

The South is not unconscious of its problem. Southerners
have been putting the question in various forms. Should the
South, they ask, become a replica of the industrialized North,
with all the advantages and disadvantages that go with that
way of life? Or does the South have something essential and
unique which is worth preserving? Does Birmingham want
to be another Pittsburgh, Richmond another Chicago, Raleigh another Newark, or Charleston another Detroit?

Margaret Coit in her biography of John C. Calhoun states
the problem as she sees it:

"Whether the South of today, in the throes of warborn
prosperity, will sacrifice the remaining values of its way of
life by accepting the industrial democracy against which Calhoun fought, or whether it can, at last, work out a new life,
holding the good of its dream, untainted by either the dark
stain of slavery or of industrial tyranny, is perhaps America's
foremost problem. Ironically enough, it is at the very mo-

ment when the weaknesses of industrial democracy which revolted Calhoun are at last becoming apparent to those who live under the system that it is only too likely to be embraced by the Carolinian's fellow countrymen."

The implication here is that "the dark stain of industrial tyranny" is inevitable in industrialization. However, that is not certain; industrial democracy may overcome industrial tyranny, as it appears to be doing in America today. Furthermore if "the weaknesses of industrial democracy which revolted Calhoun" are becoming apparent to those who live under it, it is arguable that the people will correct them, and this too is happening.

Of course it is possible that the New South will embrace the new industrialism with the uncritical fervor of a fresh convert and will try to outdo the North at it. Already Southerners are boasting that some Southern chemical plants are so automatic that they practically run themselves. But it is probable that industry will suffer a considerable sea-change in crossing the Potomac and will adapt itself in large measure to the Southern way of life, becoming more rural and more neighborly.

Illustrations of the South's skepticism regarding the *deus ex machina* are not hard to find. This agnosticism became practically sacrilegious in the blasts which emanated from the Fugitive-Agrarian group in Tennessee in the 1920's, culminating in the symposium by a dozen Southern writers in 1930 entitled *I'll Take My Stand*. This work was issued as a challenge to "a monolithic culture of unredeemed materialism" and was based on the premise that "the South, with its inherited institutions and its system of values, was a continuation of Western European culture, and that the North was the deviation."

This group in general looked on industrialism as "an insidious spirit, full of false promises and generally fatal to establishments . . . a menial of almost miraculous cunning but no intelligence" which "needs to be strongly governed or it will destroy the economy of the household."

Some twenty years later the group had disintegrated, but most of its members were still taking the same old stand. One of them, H. C. Nixon, saw more danger than ever in "a Southern worship of industrial gods and economic progress, with no little disregard of our traditional values in an atmosphere of technological illiteracy." The South, he feared, was about to accept industrialism as its master instead of its slave, and to lose "the art of living" in an overpowering emphasis on developing "the art of getting a living . . . We are developing experts and 'go-getters' but running into a shortage of whole men to sustain the heritage of a Jefferson, a Madison, or a John Taylor of Caroline."

The Agrarians were not opposed to industry "in its place," though, to be sure, they did not consider that place a prominent one. Frank L. Owsley, their leader in so far as these individualists had a leader, envisioned the agrarian spirit, opposed to the industrial spirit, as one in which agriculture would be the leading vocation, "whether for wealth, pleasure or prestige," to be pursued "with intelligence and leisure." In such a society, he prophesied, "the old communities, the old churches, the old songs, would arise from their moribund slumbers. Art, music and literature would emerge into the sunlight from the dark, cramped holes where industrial insecurity and industrial insensitiveness have driven them. There would be a sound basis for statesmanship to take the place of demagoguery and corrupt politics. Leisure and good manners and the good way of life might again become ours."

Maybe so and maybe not. Southerners have had ample proof in the past hundred years that demagogues and farmers, corrupt politics and the rural way of life, are not incompatible. If Southerners are skeptical of the blessings of industrialism, they are doubly skeptical of agrarianism, which they call farming, because they have given it a thorough trial, and it has gotten them into the very fix from which they are desperately trying to extricate themselves. Many of them would agree with Ellen Glasgow when she said that while she was out of sympathy with the crude industrialism which has taken over parts of the South, she could "not work up any enthusiasm over a rural civilization dominated by hookworm and fundamentalism." The South is patently in no mood to abandon its new industrialism for its old agrarianism.

It is reasonable to assume that what the South wants is a balance between industry and agriculture. There is plenty of room in the South for both; the problem is to eliminate the worst and retain the best features of each.

Gerald W. Johnson posed one phase of the issue in the proper light when he wrote in *The Wasted Land:*

"The question is not, Should the South abandon its machines and factories? but, Is it now at or close to the degree of industrialization that will afford it proper maximum opportunity for the development of its capacities? . . .

"Certain sinister features of industrialism in the South can neither be denied nor defended; which does not alter the fact that a further industrial development, on socially more efficient lines, might be expected to reduce the human waste that now characterizes the region . . .

"The question before Southern industrialism is whether or not employers and employees in the Southeast will be able to profit by the experience of other regions . . .

"The Southeast can avoid the greater part of the waste of industrial warfare. There is no assurance that it will; but it can."

The South has experienced some of these "sinister features"—sweatshops of low wages and long hours, the mill village in the hands of incompetent or irresponsible owners. It has observed others at longer range—the subservience of men to things, the tie-up between gangsters and corrupt politicians, the impersonality of the man-swarm of the metropolis where a person may live and die without ever knowing his neighbor's name.

The South rightly fears the tendency of industrialism to funnel human beings, as Lewis Mumford puts it, "into centers that become ever more congested and expensive to run ... with insufficient parks, playgrounds, private gardens, with expensive and time-wasting transportation systems that take people daily from congested homes where they had rather not live to equally dismal factories and offices where they had rather not work."

The South is fortunate that it is not caught in that web— not yet. Its civilization is still fluid, more rural than urban, it has not hardened into a set pattern; its towns and cities still have an opportunity to grow in grace as well as in size. "What we need to know," says Rupert B. Vance in *The Human Geography of the South*, "is that, in spite of its tragic history, the mold in which the South needs to be fashioned is only now being laid." The South has a good chance to evade the darker aspects of industrialization and urbanization which have plagued other regions.

That outsiders as well as Southerners realize this is indicated by what James H. Gray said after moving from Massachusetts to Albany, Georgia to edit a newspaper there:

"The veteran is turning South with increasing numbers of his comrades because living is more friendly, is less complex and is more open to individual expression than the sections where industrial centers predominate. The South in particular has a very special goal at which to aim. It has the stuff with which to create an environment that is far removed from the sterile, fundamentally indecent manifestations of an industrial society. It can give dignity and renewed moral strength to the workingman, who has suffered nothing but frustration and negation in the great crowded cities constructed, not for man's benefit, but for the perpetuation of the voracious mechanical-industrial cycle. In short, the South, through its prosperous communal life, based comfortably on small industry allied closely with agriculture, can teach men how to master and live in ease with his mechanical marvels. This is the appeal of the South for me. That is why I am here."

The South is fortunate also that, since it must be industrialized, it has the latest models of industry to choose from. These are vastly improved over the depressing and dangerous models of 1850, 1900 or even 1930.

The Northern "wage-slaves" of Timrod's polemic poetry have evolved into independent and self-respecting workers who know their worth and with the aid of their unions generally get it. Conditions of labor are incomparably better than they were a few decades ago. The old mill village has a new face. A great many of the new manufacturing plants are being built, not in the city or even the town, but in the country; a large proportion of the workers not only own their cars, but also their own homes in the country with a garden or even a farm to go with them. A model town called Appliance Park, outside Louisville, Kentucky, for the workers in the tremendous new General Electric manufacturing plant, is being constructed by the company in accordance with the advice of city planners and landscape architects. This is an extreme illustration of what industrialism can do for the South.

Another illustration may be found in the advertisement of the Du Pont textile plant at Kinston, North Carolina, which promises its workers: security (steady, year-around employment with no seasonal breaks), fair wages (approximately

$50 a week to start, with increases as earned), opportunity
(training program to qualify workers for increased earnings),
pleasant work place (new, modern plant, medical department
and cafeteria), and employee benefit plan (wages when sick,
free life insurance, vacations with pay and company-paid
Blue Cross insurance for eligible employees).

The days when big corporations, in the nearly absolute
control of uneducated and irresponsible men, ground the last
drop of sweat from their employees before throwing them on
the scrap heap, are gone, perhaps forever and certainly for the
time being, and the South in process of being industrialized
is lucky that it is so. The modern corporation may not have
acquired a soul, but it has developed intelligence and a sense
of social responsibility; it has had some sense knocked into
its head. "The tycoon is dead," *Fortune* Magazine asserts.
"The mid-century businessman has had to go to school—in
labor, in politics, in social welfare. The engineer's a businessman, the salesman's an economist, the research man knows
advertising, the finance man knows law." Business has become professionalized. The really big businessman today is
likely to be an engineer or a lawyer; the new crop of mana-
gers are products of schools of business administration and
have been exposed to more university enlightenment than
was dreamed of in the nightmares of their rugged-individual-
istic elders.

Indeed, the sociological qualities of industry in America
have been changing so fast that the critic who draws back his
arm to cast a stone at her is liable to be embarrassed to find
that she has changed from a scarlet woman to a pillar of the
ladies' aid society while he was winding up.

The economic democracy which American industry has
been practicing increasingly has lifted millions of people
from poverty to middle-class comfort and luxury. America,

as Frederick Lewis Allen points out in *The Big Change,* has discovered a new economic frontier, "the purchasing power of the poor." Therefore it is "not evolving *toward* socialism but *past* socialism." This has been accomplished "through a combination of patchwork revisions of the system—tax laws, minimum wage laws, subsidies and guarantees and regulations of various sorts, plus labor union pressures and new management attitudes."

If Karl Marx and Henry B. Timrod could come back to earth, they would be amazed to find that the working man in the United States has attained an unexampled degree of freedom, comfort and prosperity. Marx would be shocked from center to circumference to learn that one of the firmest foundations of his philosophy—the supposed inability of capitalism to reform itself—has been shot out from under him, since the American capitalistic system has proved that the American laborer can gain very great material benefits without the state ownership of industry which would be perilous alike to his life and property.

What application does this have to the South? It means that the South is being industrialized at a time when industry has attained not only a new efficiency but a new sense of social responsibility, and when city planning is a technique by which cities, instead of degenerating into blighted areas and slums, can grow in convenience, comfort and beauty as well as size. There is a new spirit abroad in the South which is building modern factories in ancient cotton fields. "The Old South of the rotting plantation houses, a wretched single-crop agriculture, the share-cropper living in a mud-plastered cabin," as Louis Bromfield observes, "is rapidly becoming more obsolete than the slave economy on which it rested." The South is no longer inhibited by what Arnold J. Toynbee calls "the nemesis of creativity: idolization of the ephemeral self."

In brief, the contemplation of the navel of its once glorious past is no longer the South's chief occupation.

With the aid of diversified industry, the South is fast closing the gap between it and the American standard of living. Simultaneously it is putting its mark on the industry which has come to it and which is closer to nature than it was in the North. The South, with its new resources, wealth and surprising capacity for home-grown, sociological research, is in a position to create a finer, kindlier, happier and more beautiful way of life than it—or perhaps any other region—has yet known. There is no assurance that it will, but it can.

The "not quite immovable object" is being moved—far and fast.

# 16

## Challenge and Response

Under the impact of new forces the South will move in new directions. It will produce more goods and acquire more wealth. But that is not saying what it will become.

These are material matters, and the South has never been explained by materialism—dialectical or otherwise. The material forces will act on a rather peculiar people, with minds, ways and wills of their own.

The South, as it becomes more standardized and Americanized, is in effect re-entering the Union, and it will take a more responsible and effective part in it than it has done in a long time.

It is coming back in a period of history when the survival of its nation and its civilization is challenged by powerful forces of decadence inside and aggression outside.

The South has never been backward about accepting a challenge. This challenge, however, is more subtle than most —it is not so much physical as mental and spiritual. The question is what, if anything, the South, has to contribute within the national framework.

What, more precisely, is the challenge? In America, it

springs from a confusion of mind and a weakening of moral fiber, which are caused by a civilization overintent on material rewards, and which result in a lack of adherence to ethical standards by both businessmen and politicians, together with an absence of that highest quality of leadership which America has somehow, in its gravest crises of the past, found in its great men—in Washington, Lincoln, Wilson. Abroad, the challenge is one of recurrent aggression resulting in a series of world wars—the day before yesterday by a monarchy, yesterday by fascism-nazism, today by communism—waged with weapons of ever increasing devastation and pointing clearly to the destruction of urban civilization.

America's strength, complemented by Europe's weakness, has thrust a reluctant United States of America into the role of leadership of the free nations in this chronic crisis, but America's wisdom has not yet justified that leadership or made it effective in a world of guided missiles and unguided sovereign states.

Unfortunately, in this critical period, the impression which millions of Europeans and Asiatics have gotten of America, however falsely, is that it is a land of bubblegum, yo-yos, jukeboxes, lynchings, tight sweaters, loose morals, diamond-studded gangsters and mink-coated gun molls. After seeing American B-grade moving pictures which have flooded the earth from Tokyo to Casablanca, they are intrigued with our preoccupation with violence; while they observe that virtue always triumphs because the hero is a split-second quicker on the draw than the villain, they wonder whether that is all America has to say to them about problems which are far too deep and complex to be solved by violence alone. In brief, they see that we have a giant's strength, but are not convinced that we will use it as a wise man. As a result, we have been shocked time and again to see nations which, if only in self-defense, should be our friends and allies, turn away from us. We think we have lost their friendship, whereas in fact we have lost something more vital—their trust in our ability to solve the life and death problems of our time.

This trust will be restored, if at all, by something more than goods or arms. Whether America will call effectively upon its reserves of wisdom—which ought to be pretty full by now since they have remained undepleted of late—is the question.

Such are the requirements of the problem. Woodrow Wilson referred to a similar situation when he said ". . . the greatest nation is the nation that penetrates to the heart of its duty and mission among the nations of the world. With every insight into the great policies of mankind, the nation that has that vision is elevated to a place of influence and power which it cannot get by arms, which it cannot get by commercial rivalry, which it can get in no other way than by that spiritual leadership which comes from a profound understanding of the problems of humanity. . . ."

Dr. Charles Malik of Lebanon expressed the same truth, which America needs most to recognize, when he said in an address to the Political Committee of the United Nations in 1949:

"If your only export in these realms is the silent example of flourishing political institutions and happy human relations, you cannot lead. Nor can you really lead if you send forth to others only expert advice and technical assistance. To be able to lead and save yourself and others, you must above everything else address their mind and soul. Your tradition, rooted in the glorious Graeco-Roman-Hebrew-Christian-Western-European-humane outlook, supplies you with all the necessary presuppositions for leadership. All you have to do is to be the deepest you really are."

What contribution can the South make to national leadership in this troubled and perilous time?

This question does not imply that the South has any unique contribution arising from monopoly of virtue or that we are the people and wisdom will die with us. But it does imply that the South, at its best, may have certain useful traits and tendencies created partly by heredity and partly by an environment in which some Southerners may have learned some lessons better in adversity than others have in prosperity.

First, Southerners—not all of them, but some of them—have learned, the hard way, to be skeptical of the materialism which has increasingly fastened on the country since 1865. They have had ample opportunity thrust on them to sit back and observe what it did to others. They appreciate the truth of Toynbee's paradoxical axiom, culled from his study of history, that "nothing fails like worldly success." It was a Southern writer, Thomas Wolfe, who wrote, "I believe we are lost here in America, but I believe we shall be found," and who named the enemy "compulsive greed." Of course, many Southerners will fall down and worship "the bitch goddess, Success," but others, while not inhospitable to her, will refuse to bow the knee, and will remember how Aeschylus said that it seems to be a law of life that "those who learn must suffer" and that "against our will and in our own despite, wisdom comes to us by the awful grace of God."

Second, the South is not known as the "Bible Belt" for nothing. With all its narrowness, bigotry, hypocrisy and plain tomfoolery in religious matters, it does, again at its best, have a fierce attachment to righteousness which is a power in itself and which is not found everywhere. William Alexander Percy expressed it well, when he wrote in his *Lanterns on the Levee,* during the Second World War when a Nazi victory appeared inevitable:

Should I therefore teach deceit, dishonor, ruthlessness, bestial force to the children in order that they survive? Better that they perish. It is sophistry to speak of two sets of virtues; there is but one; virtue is an end in itself; the survival virtues are means, not ends. Honor and honesty, compassion and truth are good even if they kill you, for they alone give life its dignity and worth. . . . Probably those that practice virtue will be destroyed, but it is better for men to die than to call evil good, and virtue will never die.

William Faulkner touched the same note:

McCaslin watched him, still speaking, the voice, the words as quiet as twilight itself, was: 'Courage and honor and pride and pity and love of justice and of liberty. They all touch the heart, and what the heart holds to becomes the truth. Do you see now?'

Does that sound like Faulkner? Well, it is Faulkner, and it is the voice of the South.

Third, the South—which was doing business before the Union was—may have worth-while insights into the nature and purpose of the Union it helped form. While some Southerners know very well that the hallmark of America is freedom, that her symbols are the Liberty Bell and the Statue of Liberty, and that her machinery for maintaining freedom is the Constitution, they know also that freedom is not an end in itself but a means whereby each person should have the chance to develop all the excellence in him, that Americans are not free for nothing, but for something—to pursue truth, do good, create beauty. They would agree with Gerald W. Johnson that "free speech is for bold people; freedom of conscience is for reasonable people; free enterprise is for honest people; freedom of inquiry is for hopeful people; freedom of association is for steady people; states' rights are for energetic people; freedom of opportunity is for great people." They realize that America is suffering from a

Faustian preoccupation with materialism, "which talks of freedom and is slave to riches," at a time when America must undertake the moral, as well as the military, leadership of Western Civilization, and while America is still trying to strike the proper balance between freedom and discipline, equality and excellence, materialism and idealism. It is a large order.

Assuming that the South, at its best, possesses these traits and insights, what specific contributions can it make?

1. It can take steps to solve, or mitigate, its race problem, in a more humane and democratic fashion than it has yet done.

2. It can once more try sending its best men to represent it in Washington. Since 1865, it has tried sending its worst, and later its mediocre men, but there was a time when its best—Washington, Jefferson, Madison—were very good. The time has come for the South to send its best again.

3. The South can address its best intellectual effort to contributing to the solution of the central problem of our time. That problem is war. Civilization cannot stand an indefinite series of world wars any more than a man can stand an indefinite number of paralytic strokes. Western Civilization is rapidly teaching its own destruction; a short time ago the Chinese did not know how to fight and the Russians did not know how to make long-range bombers; they know now. Two thousand years ago the West imported religion from the East; tomorrow, if things continue on their present course, it will import exploding H-bombs.

Our civilization appears to have only three courses open to it: destruction, world domination, or world peace. Destruction would be accomplished in one of two ways: swiftly by atomic bombs, or slowly by the attrition of ever increasing armaments, the total world cost of which already exceeds some $110,000,000,000 a year or not less than one-eighth of the world's production; the question being whether civilization will go out with a bang or a whimper.

World domination by one nation is the second possibility in a shrunken, frightened world; the Soviet Union might come to it avidly, the United States of America reluctantly. If the peoples of the world cannot find peace in freedom, they will seek it in tyranny. They want to live.

World peace through world law is the third possibility. Tragically, it appears to be the most remote of the three. The only answer to world war is world law, but this involves some form of world government in a world hell-bent on unrestricted national governments. The problem is to create a world government strong enough to keep the peace, but so limited that it will be prevented from interfering in the domestic affairs of its member nations. Theoretically and technically, the problem is not unsolvable; the American Founding Fathers solved a basically similar problem when they drafted the Constitution of the United States. But the practical difficulties of applying this solution on a world scale under existing circumstances are so vast and complex as to be almost insurmountable.

Notwithstanding, the South, on its return to the Union, might well direct its political genius, as it did in the days of Madison, to the creation of peace by law among sovereign states.

# ACKNOWLEDGMENT

Writers of poems, short stories, and essays get no help or sympathy, but when anyone writes a book he is the beneficiary of a tradition whereby busy and expert people drop what they are doing and come to his aid with information, advice and criticism.

I have been greatly helped by this wonderful tradition in writing this book. Although I cannot even count those who have helped me with gifts of their time and energy, there are certain persons to whom I want to give special thanks:

To Dr. Howard W. Odum of Chapel Hill, N. C., for reading the manuscript and making helpful suggestions;

To James Street, Professors Albert Coates, Rupert B. Vance, Samuel Selden, Benjamin Swalin, and John Allcott of Chapel Hill; Professor George P. Wilson, A. L. Brooks, Esq., and Haywood Duke of Greensboro; Rufus Terral, of the St. Louis Post-Dispatch, and Marion Brown of Burlington, for advice on certain chapters;

To Dr. Clarence Poe of Raleigh and Julius Smith, Esq., of Greensboro, for letters of introduction;

To H. M. Conway, Jr., director of the Southern Association of Science and Industry at Atlanta, to the research departments of the Federal Reserve Banks and to the Manufacturers Record of Baltimore, for information on the economic development of the South;

To Judge E. E. Rives of Greensboro, J. Edgar Hoover, director of the Federal Bureau of Investigation, and to his *Uniform Crime Reports,* for help with the chapter on violence in the South;

To Gerald W. Johnson of Baltimore for suggesting to the publisher that I ought to write a book on the South, though there have been times during the writing when thanks would have stuck in my throat;

To Frances Phillips and Helen King, editors of William Morrow and Company, publishers, for wise, patient and unfailing encouragement, guidance and criticism;

To Samuel Stoney for showing me that marvelous part of the South which is Charleston;

To the Library of the Woman's College of the University of North Carolina at Greensboro; to the Greensboro Public Library, and especially to Olivia Burwell, head librarian, and Irene Hester, reference librarian;

To my wife, Marion, who bore with me and stuck by me during the writing; to Isabel Parris, secretary of the editorial department of the *Greensboro Daily News,* who typed the manuscript and encouraged me; to Carl O. Jeffress, general manager of the Greensboro News Company, who gave me time off when I needed it; and to my colleagues, H. W. Kendall, editor, and William D. Snider, associate editor of the *Greensboro Daily News,* who took on my editorial duties when I was off working on the book.

WILLIAM T. POLK

*Greensboro, N. C.*
*Aug. 1, 1953.*

NCLM